MW01297125

"This profound and beautifully-written book will forever change your understanding not only of whales but of the possible depth of communion that all of us can enjoy with nature. The future of the planet depends on millions of us awakening now to this communion and to enacting the kinds of protection that will ensure our continued life together. I congratulate Diane on her superb work and on the courage it took to share her discoveries with us so nakedly and simply."

Andrew Harvey, author of *The Hope* and *Savage Grace*.

"In this luminous volume, Diane Knoll takes us into the heart of the mystery that is the sea and its most majestic inhabitant, the whale. She brings to her task the soul of a seeker, rather than the objective scrutiny of the investigator. What ensues is thus a moving and poetic account of initiation into a secret world unguessed at by the many. Her personal odyssey becomes a universal depiction of discovery and joy, of revelation and exaltation as her narrative unfolds. This is a book to be read and treasured by anyone who cares about the possibilities of communion between species and rapturous immersion into the wonders of nature."

Dorothy Walters, PHD, *Some Kiss We Want: Poems Selected and New; Unmasking the Rose: An Account of a Kundalini Initiation.*

"Blasted my heart open" is a phrase used in *Mysticism & Whales* more than once. Yet it never becomes trite because we delude ourselves if we believe we can engage in a spiritual journey without such an experience- or many. The journey consists of numerous sacred encounters, and we further delude ourselves if we think these can happen only with humans. Diane Knoll nakedly shares her sacred encounters with whales and the life-altering, soul altering transformations they birthed in her world. Our indigenous elders were intimately familiar with such animal epiphanies and experienced them regularly. If members of the so-called civilized modernity were open to reconnecting with themselves, with each other, and with Earth with the willingness Knoll demonstrates in *Mysticism & Whales*, we would be living on a transformed planet that bears no resemblance to this one. I bow to the blessed whales and to Knoll who took me deeper into their watery world than I could have imagined.

Carolyn Baker, author of *Dark Gold: The Human Shadow and The Global Crisis* and co-author with Andrew Harvey of *Savage Grace* and *Return to Joy*.

Mysticism
& Whales

Mysticism & Whales

A PILGRIMAGE

Diane Knoll

© 2017 Diane Knoll
All rights reserved.

ISBN: 1978209045
ISBN 13: 9781978209046
Library of Congress Control Number: 2017915996
CreateSpace Independent Publishing Platform
North Charleston, South Carolina

To
My husband Jon,
The beautiful people of Argentina,
and of course
The sacred beings of the sea,
The Whales

Contents

§

Photographs

Introduction

§

Everything is laid out for you.
Your path is straight ahead of you.
Sometimes it's invisible but it's there.
You may not know where it's going,
But you have to follow that path.
It's the path to the Creator.
It's the only path there is.

—CHIEF LEON SHENANDOAH[1]

THE NATIVE AMERICAN SHAMAN SAID, "Come. The whales are calling."

Sick, despondent, numb, a thread pulled with a tug that could not be ignored. I longed to the healed. I said "Yes" through the fear and the unknown as I boarded a plane to the Southern Hemisphere.

Buenos Aires opened her arms in welcome. After a few days of exploring the city we took a two-hour flight south to Trelew, a Patagonian town on the Atlantic Ocean. Driving north for another hour and a half, at times on gravel road, we traveled to Piramides, a small sea village on the Peninsula Valdes.

In the wide open space of the arid steppe it is easy to imagine gauchos riding for days without seeing another human. The vast expanse of physical space echoes the boundless sacred expansion many of us experience on this pilgrimage. As we enter into the Nature Preserve on the peninsula, the Southern Right Whales await us.

This unexpected, joyous, tumultuous dance with the whales catapulted me out of my conservative world into a South American tango with Creation. The whales, the sea, the land, and the sky have opened my soul. My life has been transformed and the transformation continues, as it has for many of the others who followed this path. Unexpected, magnificent, powerful, and blessed, we walk differently since experiencing the embrace of the whales and Creation.

This is our story.

PART ONE

Whales and Creation—
Sacred Discoveries

§

One day you finally knew
what you had to do, and began...

—Mary Oliver[2]

CHAPTER 1

The Soul's Cry—A Journey to Transformation

§

You wake up in the morning consumed by an urge to get
on with it. What "it" is, you do not know, but it is barking
at your heels like the Hounds of Heaven. Something
unknown is calling you, and you know you will cross
continents, oceans—realities even—to discover it.

—JEAN HOUSTON[3]

MY SOUL FILLED WITH A yearning, a longing for wholeness, for meaning,
for God. It could not be stopped. It could not be ignored. I was pulled by
an intensity that demanded an answer. Victor Frankel's words, "striving
to find meaning in one's life is the primary motivational force in man
[*sic*]"[4] and Matthew Fox's statement, "What is needed in overdeveloped
peoples is a liberation of the mystic."[5] inspired me. I said "Yes" to a search
for meaning by entering into the mysteries, experiencing God, and discovering liberation. I have indeed crossed continents, oceans, and realities.

The mystic's journey, pilgrimage, or call to awaken requires letting go of structures, beliefs, and behaviors that have formed a safe

cocoon and often a prison for the soul. The courage to step outside of the known, predictable, and linear mechanical world view is essential. Poets and saints, the sacred scriptures, legends and myths proclaim the necessity of this surrender. Our soul's cry is to be heard, seen, loved, and useful. When it seems that the way has been lost, stepping into the unknown is an opening to grace.

The call of the whales became my step into the unknown.

CHAPTER 2

Opening to Connection—A Pilgrimage to the Whales

§

A part of the world that seems to resist domestication,
Patagonia is on good terms with the wind, whales, penguins
and waves, but puts the endurance of the human spirit to
the test. It may be considered as one of the uttermost parts
of the Earth, or, perhaps, as the origin of an adventure.

—LICHTER AND CAMPAGNA[6]

THE ADVENTURE BEGAN IN SOUTH America. Becoming like Hildegard's "feather on the breath of God"[7] I traveled to Patagonia to be with the Southern Right Whales, *Eubalaena australis,* who come to the Peninsula Valdes in Argentina from May until December to mate, give birth, and nurse their calves. I went, not as a binocular-holding voyeur, but in an indigenous way with listening and respect.

I began my life journey as a proper robot, conforming with excellence and precision to society's expectations. Becoming empty and exhausted I collapsed. The nutrients were missing. I could not survive. Something bigger, something deeper was pulling me. I knew it involved the sacred but I had no idea where to find it. I looked at my conventional world and it was not there. If not there, where? After a long period of darkness, a power grasped me, leading me, cajoling me in a dance choreographed with exquisite beauty. The steps have been unexpected and unknown, containing swoops, turns, and spins. Each step, even though sometimes dark, painful, or silent has, in retrospect, been guided by grace and has contained a beautiful rhythm that seemed to be the rhythm of the universe.

The moment my certain and predictable life broke open I could never return to who I had been. I was exposed to something real that seemed totally unknown to me. It wasn't unknown, of course, only forgotten. It is as if my traditional education had imposed limits rather than continuing to offer expansion. With a Phi Beta Kappa key, by most Western standards I would be considered quite educated. Perhaps therein lies the problem. I was considered educated *by Western standards*. My true education was, in fact, just beginning.

CHAPTER 3

Meeting the Whales

§

Nothing will ever mean as much to a person as seeing a whale
close-at-hand in the wild. That is something you never forget.

—ROGER PAYNE[8]

I WAS TOLD BY A Native American woman that I would receive a mother's nurturing embrace from the whales. Thinking that sounded good,
although somewhat unlikely, I walked along the crescent beach of the
Patagonian shore for the first time. Reaching the water's edge I looked
out. A large whale came towards me. I stood in awe as I felt my body
melt and soften. My heart felt as if it had golden streams of light radiating out as it opened to the whale. Tears fell. I was loved.

So what would this Western woman from the Pacific Northwest do
with this experience? How to explain this profound first meeting? It fit
none of the parameters of life I had been taught. It made no sense, yet it
was so. My body knew. My mind just needed a new frame of reference.
The frame became one that I could not map out, predict, or control. I
was invited and welcomed into a new world, one that would challenge
and upset almost all of what I had previously been taught, the rules I
had followed, and in fact my very being. Who I was would never be the

same. Of course I didn't know all of that then. All I knew was that I was loved. It was a love bigger than anything I could have imagined.

The next day I went out on a boat to see the whales. A single whale circled us. I saw her. I am to remember her, remember being held and enveloped. There is a circle of protection around me. The whale came to me, blasting open the tightness, entering me. My breath quivered with exquisite desire. I was known. The bands that held me released in wonder. The whale once again made me cry. From deep inside the tears came with relief, melting my frozenness. I watched then as her calf emerged. The mother covered her baby—safe, warm and held, gentle, strong, there. And then from her safety came the courage to play. Splash, jump, twirl. Always mama waited, steady, so the baby could be free.

Beautiful lessons of protection and freedom. The whales opened my body, connecting me to something so much bigger than what I am in isolation. The energy tingled, bubbling through me. I felt steadier, stronger, larger. The golden, warm love washed over me, melting my heart as tears of joy streamed down my face.

CHAPTER 4

The Call of Creation

§

We come to understand that what is reflected by nature is
not just who we are now but also who we could become.
And so we begin entering nature as a pilgrim in search
of his true home, a wanderer with an intimation of
communion, a solitary with a suspicion of salvation.

—BILL PLOTKIN[9]

PULLING, THROBBING, INSISTENT, AND UNRELENTING—A power called
me and I surrendered; it was calling me to authenticity, immersing me
in nature. The power of the Earth, lost for so long in our culture began
my healing. I learned to celebrate, seeing my spiritual journey woven
with the same magnificent, numinous threads as the cosmos. Nature
became my lover and my teacher, awakening me to participate in the
grand adventure of Creation.

Living in the North American Pacific Northwest I am surrounded
by mountains, trees, and water—truly glorious and abundant—yet I
had become so busy, so linear and literal that I could not see the beauty
around me. I was asked to go to the opposite end of the Earth so that I
could be removed from all that was keeping me blind and closed. I would
open to awe on the South American Patagonian coast of Argentina.

This removal from the known to the unknown, from civilization to the wilderness, from noise to quiet, allows the soul the space of contemplation, creativity, and transformation. Nature embraces, teaches, and supports the exhausted, floundering heart, showing a different rhythm and an expanded home. Walking in the luminous power and beingness of Creation we become free to be.

It is a surprise to discover how very far away from our being we have been living. Most of us live as if we are not part of the ecosystem. The folly of human dominance has kept us separate and undernourished. Attempting to fill our hunger and emptiness, humans began a relentless cycle of production and consumption, greed and exploitation.

When we meet ourselves in nature, we can begin the adventure of discovering who we really are and also who we can become. We can learn to discard what we no longer need; just as the trees lose their leaves and the flowers their petals, we discover that the possibility of letting go exists for us as well. We can grow. Change is possible. We do not need to stay struck by hanging on to what has deadened us. Mutation can occur. It is the way of Creation and the hope for us.

We are not machines in a cosmic world only able to look longingly at the fluidity and splendor of nature. We belong. We are not alone. We are not separate. We are part of the elegant unfolding of the universe.

CHAPTER 5

Hidden and Seen— Sacred Encounters

§

Surrender, even to the divine, is something our culture does
not encourage. Surrender to the divine means crossing over
from our well-defined roles and worlds into the realm of the
gods, where everything is possible and nothing is explained.
We have no idea what to expect and so we are afraid.

—ROBERT A. JOHNSON[10]

How MUCH OF LIFE IS spent hiding behind a mask? A body that is doing one thing, a mind another, and emotions another, while the exterior
is plastic and false as it tries to hide the interior activities. Hiding has
become a way of life. Our interior simmers, a cauldron bubbling with
creative potential, yet we are so often numb we do not even know this
powerful interior exists, and sadly we live life as a dull imitation of what
could be.

Why do we hide? We think we are in control. It feels safer. It is all
we know. Nothing much excites us so we do as we are told. We follow
the rules. We are good people, industrious hard-working people. It does

not occur to us, at least very often, to even question if the rules make sense, or if the hard work is important or making a difference. So the deadening complacency and boredom creep in, covering us with what seem to be impenetrable layers. We slog along, trying to make the best of life in the only way we know how. What can overturn this hiding? How can the interior passion emerge to be felt, seen, and lived?

This is the purpose of a sacred encounter. A shell is shattered and the pulsating interior radiates outward, free and uncontained. A throbbing joy, hitherto unknown emerges, connecting to the Divine in radiant wholeness, radiant holiness.

Sacred encounters are often unexpected. Creation offers an invitation and something deep inside says "Yes" before the mind can plan, organize, wonder, and worry. The longing for wholeness resoundingly says "Yes" and probably also says, "It's about time." Sacred encounters come in a myriad of ways; the key is to follow through with the Yes, not to smother it with logic, fear, and practicality. For me it was the whales, in another culture, using another language, incredibly far from my home. I was a pilgrim on a pilgrimage. Something was waiting to be broken open. The Divine called.

In the presence of the power, energy, and magnificence of a whale the hiding dissolves. It is no longer possible to hold up the screen, the armor, the covering. The sacred thrusts through, uniting with our own divinity, exploding, penetrating the separation. This has been the experience of many of us with the whales—no longer able to hide—we are both vulnerable and expansively powerful. Energetically zapped and charged, we have been changed.

CHAPTER 6

Taught by the South

§

To love means to listen.

—THICH NHAT HANH[11]

A common communicator between the northern
hemisphere and the southern hemisphere—the whale.

—FRED GRAHAM[12]

WHEN I SET FOOT IN South America for the first time I felt a warmth
that was nearly liquid engulf me. What was this feeling that was new,
yet remembered as complete and right? I have traveled to many places
around the globe but standing in Buenos Aires I entered a world that
seemed beautifully embracing and very different from what I had been
living in and what I was used to.

Feeling almost drugged, I knew I had to immerse myself in this
softness. When I asked my Native American teacher, "What is this?
What is happening?" she said that North America is a place of the head
and South America is a place of the heart. Now I was experiencing what
my heart had been longing for.

My South American teacher then said words that have become one of my beacons of light. She said, "It is so amazing that you came here wanting to learn from us. People from the North always want to come to teach us, they rarely want to learn from us." So I found myself in Argentina with the whales, knowing that I must learn.

Why does the North, the place of power and wealth and control always talk and want to teach, rarely wanting to listen and learn? What is the threat of not having an answer, not knowing, not being in control? Why do we not want to learn? Why do we think that only we have wisdom?

We have colonized, tried to destroy sacred teachings and ways of life, marginalized cultures, and attempted to repress the nourishing embrace, the receptivity, wisdom and power of the sacred feminine that flourished outside of the patriarchal power and control of the North.

It is time for this to stop. It is time to learn. It is time to open. The drive for power, control, and wealth is destroying the world.

I am so grateful for the message. I am listening and being taught by ways different from driven, materialistic, cold, rational control. I am learning to open to warmth, fluidity, and awe. The South and the whales have taught what all my academic work and will power to accumulate success could only hint at.

Each culture has something to teach. We are a bouquet with the splendor of every culture as a flower adding to the beauty of the whole. I know now that if we refuse to listen, we become part of the destruction of what could have blossomed. We sever the thread of connection, something that leaves us all in isolation. When we shut our ears and use our voices in pontification we drown the song of the universe.

Listening is essential for peace.

CHAPTER 7

Loco?

§

The truly wise person
kneels at the feet of all creatures
and is not afraid to endure
the mockery of others.

—MECHTILD OF MAGDEBURG[13]

WE WALK AND TALK, WORK and play in a literal, tangible world. What is it about whales that captures the hearts of people, people who have considered themselves normal, scientific even? What is the strength of this call? A call people all over the world hear. Some of us answer that call. Is it indescribable? Perhaps.

In a conversation conducted in Spanish with the owner of one of the whale watching operations in Piramides, Argentina, we talked about the spiritual connection we have with the whales and used the Spanish word *loco* (crazy), thinking that we might seem like that to him as a business-man. His face softened as he looked at us and quietly said, "No, not *loco*. Every year my family leaves me and then they return." The Southern Right Whales leave the Peninsula Valdes in December and return in May. They are part of his family as they are part of mine.

Explainable to the Western world? Not easily. But the indigenous people know. They have known since ancient times. They pray *Mitakuye Oyasin,* All My Relations, knowing that all of Creation is related. The whales are indeed family.

Many of us are now remembering.

What seems crazy to one culture can be truth to another. The question might be which view brings connection, connection to each other and to Creation? Which view brings fullness and compassion and joy?

The indigenous people say, "Whale carries the history of Mother Earth."[14] and "Whale signals a time of finding your origins, of seeing your overall destiny as coded in your DNA."[15] They also state that "Whale is linked with movement and change at a most profound level. With whale's global connections, this suggests something that could affect all of humankind . . . connecting with higher planes of consciousness."[16]

In the presence of whales, the history in these ancient beings and the global significance of the connection is reality. Letting go of individual languages and nationalities and even species differentiation, one enters into an expanded level of consciousness. We who have been with the whales in Argentina call it *becoming enwhaled.*

CHAPTER 8

A Cathedral of Sacred Space

§

We call upon the earth, our planet home, with its beautiful
depths and soaring heights, its vitality and abundance of life,
and together we ask that it
Teach us, and show us the Way.

—CHINOOK BLESSING LITANY[17]

THE CLIFFS SOAR TOWARDS THE sky, dropping sharply into the sea with
layers of embedded, petrified shells, whale bones and stones, millions
and millions of years old. This small sea village, Puerto Piramides, set
in the midst of the magnificent cliffs, reflects an alliance with the pyramids of ancient Egypt. It is a visible and deeply felt ancient sacred space.
A natural cathedral of the universe.

As the pyramid cliffs encircle us, the gulf welcomes the whales, offering protection for mating and giving birth. We too are welcomed
into this sacred space. We are protected, given an opportunity to make
sacred love with Creation, and ultimately to give birth—transforming
into our true sacred selves.

A cathedral, in fact all truly sacred spaces, have a beauty, a power, a
grandeur that evokes silence, awe, and contemplation. In this space the

whales too become a cathedral, a deep, deep sacred space allowing us the opportunity to enter into their sacred bodies as they enter into ours. It becomes a melting together, a true communion.

Surprised by the intensity, surprised by the experience, surprised that this is even a possibility, I was shaken and I was in love. How could this be? I fell in love with God and Creation through a whale and the power of the sacred land and sea!

This cathedral experience didn't fit anything I expected or planned for. Yet it *is*.

CHAPTER 9

Praying with the Whales

§

The highest work of God is compassion.
And this means that God sets the soul
in the highest and purest place which it can occupy:
in space,
in the sea,
in a fathomless ocean,
and there
God works compassion.

—MEISTER ECKHART[18]

WE STOOD IN A CIRCLE on the boat praying a prayer of gratitude to the sun and the land for warming and embracing us, to the sea for nourishing us and its inhabitants, and to the whales. Whales have provided their bodies for food and survival, sustaining humans and making light possible. Today, many of us speak out strongly against the hunting of whales except for rare, sacred indigenous ceremonies. We no longer need their bodies for food or their oil for light. Yet we are still sustained by the whales, as they continue to bring us light, sacred light.

Praying that we continue to stay open so that we can learn what we are being asked to learn, we are invited to look around at the people in the boat, to truly see their beauty, to walk with each other in compassion and then to look outward, seeing the magnificence of Creation. Asked if anyone else would like to pray, a whale answered with a loud blow!

CHAPTER 10

The Sea

§

. . . the Spirit of God was hovering over the face of the waters.

GENESIS 1:2

WHEN WE ENTER THE SEA we become reacquainted with our primordial beginnings. The sea gives nurturance to all of her creatures and to us. The connection is strong. Many, many of us are drawn to Her sacred healing and birthing powers.

The wind kisses the sea in both gentle caresses and exuberant passion. Sometimes flat as a lake but more often swelling and dipping, the sea rocks us in the motion of a cradle. As we rest on the sea in our boat, the water can at times become rough. We can either resist and stiffen, trying to maintain our previous stability, or we can ease into the rhythm of the waves, unlocking our knees, unlocking our bodies, and move with Creation's motion. It is much less jarring to move with the water, but it does take trust. One has to relinquish perceived control. Learning to move as She does, no longer fighting against the motion but joining the dance of the waves, we become part of the sea. We surrender, surrender to what is.

Of course, there also is the honoring of the power of the sea. If the sea is too rough we stay on land, the port is closed. Watching the white caps dance is exhilarating from shore. Respecting the sea as she shows us Her power, we stand in reverence.

Water, the beautiful feminine, flows, cascading over waterfalls, down rivers, with the tides, with the wind. Not offering resistance it simply goes where it is led. Water is strong, yet fluid and surrendered. This fluid strength reminds us that to be fluid does not mean weakness.

As we watch and learn from the sea our bodies do become more fluid. It is easier somehow to become the way of the water on the sea. As we become graceful we know we are indeed filled with grace. The harder we try to step into Creation's flow, the tighter and harder we become. Trying is about will. It simply does not work. Surrendering to the flow as it courses through us, we are guided, just as the river is guided through the river bed, the waves are guided by the wind, and the tides by the moon. This surrender to connection with Creation guides powerful activity. Why is it that we think we are the guider? The sea teaches otherwise.

CHAPTER 11

Joy

§

The mystic, after all, is the divine child in us
all wanting to play in the universe.

—Matthew Fox[19]

THE WHALES SOAR UPWARD, BREAKING thought the surface of the water, reaching for the sun and then crashing down creating a glorious splash of spray that reaches toward the sky. The "ahs" burst forth from those of us in their presence. How can something so enormous move with such unbridled joy? The breathtaking leaps and breaches, magnificent tails, commanding flipper slaps, and play between the whales and their babies shower us with awe. This amazing exuberance is contagious and joy bubbles through us. It is a joy so huge that it feels as if it is bursting through every muscle and organ in our bodies.

The first year I came to Argentina and the whales, I got off the boat after an outing, walked down the dirt road in the small sea village, spread my arms out and twirled down the street. I could not contain my joy. It had to be expressed. I heard a sound and realized a table full of men, sitting at an outdoor café table, were clapping in communion with my joy! They understood. Proper, conservative me was twirling down the street with people clapping. Astounding. The joy the whales stir up is powerful indeed. The covering I had held for so long was beginning to disintegrate.

CHAPTER 12

Breath

§

To breathe deeply is to receive and that
is the feminine incarnate.

—MARION WOODMAN[20]

LEARNING TO BREATHE AGAIN, ENTERING into the breath of God is a
teaching from the whales. The sound is strong, echoing over the sea,
vibrating into our ears. Breathe.

Sacred teachings talk of breath, being breathed into life. Learning to
follow the breath, one enters into silence, clearing the noise of the mind.
Following the breath of the whale becomes a meditation, entering into
sacred spaces of expansion, freeing creative energy.

Whales are conscious breathers. Mothers teach their calves to
breathe.

"Encoded deep within the DNA of whales, there is a message:
breathe with your mother."[21] Are we also to learn to breathe with the
Great Mother, God? Yes!

As we listen to the whale's strong exhalations, our breathing slows
and deepens. A new way of being emerges. We release tightness and
constriction, discovering internal pockets of freedom and creativity
that had been unknown to us. A life of breath becomes a life lived in

meditation, breathing freedom, spouting a spray of baptism and blessing on those we encounter. This is a beautiful teaching and one of the gifts from the whales.

CHAPTER 13

Silence

§

Returning to the source is stillness, which is the way of nature.

—Lao-tsu[22]

In the presence of whales a hush falls over people. Sacred awe, so profound that it becomes the deepest of meditative silence. Even when children are present they intuitively drift into the quietest of quiet. We have entered a temple of soaring grandeur, into a sacred space that transcends all cultures, all language, and all religions. Our hearts, our bodies, our thoughts, and voices respond. It is a place of "ah" where awe dwells.

What is it about silence, this sacred hush? In this silence there is a soft gentleness. Unconsciousness drifts away and one becomes supremely conscious. This is not imposed silence that evokes an urge to rebel and make noise, this is not the cold silence of anger refusing to speak, or the awkward silence of not knowing what to say. It is the silence of reverence.

In this silence, as in all types of meditation, the clutter of life falls away, all of the details and shoulds, plans and goals dissolve. The whales and the sea absorb them. The sense of internal and external ceases. As the quiet ensues, the mind and body expand, becoming different, some-how more, deeper, wider. We are touching and being touched by awe. In this cathedral of the sea, the awe radiates into exquisite love and we are engulfed in an embrace.

CHAPTER 14

Whale Blows—A Blessing of Water

§

And for some, there is redemption, a new beginning.
Occasionally, one is baptized, washed
clean by a kind and alien eye.

—SCOTT TAYLOR[23]

THE WHALE BLOW, GLISTENING THROUGH the air, showering us with a fine mist of spray, is both a comfort and a challenge. To be blessed, anointed, baptized by a whale is a spine-tingling honor remembered for a lifetime. The mist is so fine that it encases one in a protected capsule, perhaps an egg waiting to be hatched. What will come next? All is not fairy tale bliss, however. Whale blows smell. Strong, pungent, startling. Not sweet aromatherapy, that's for sure, but aromatherapy in the truest sense. As our nose, our sinuses, our lungs inhale the eye-watering smell, we are not lulled into complacency. We startle at the olfactory assault. This is not plastic and cute; we are internally touched by something real, different, and new. What do our cells think of this touch? Although initially reacting to the smell, we then settle into it. It is as if our bodies know this is good. Just as a mother gives healing medicine to a small child who may not like the taste, perhaps the Great Mother knows the intense internal touch of the particles of water from the whale can make us well also. The awful smell becomes full of awe. We now carry in our bodies the sea and the whale.

CHAPTER 15

Sensuality

§

Friend, hope for the Guest while you are alive.
Jump into experience while you are alive!

If you make love with the divine now,
In the next life you will have the face of satisfied desire.

—KABIR[24]

THE WHALES CAME AND CAME up to me, intimately close, huge, power, recognition, and seeing. So large and encompassing. I was engulfed, totally engulfed, merged. My body released. The jacket came off, bare arms were touched by the sun and the power. Sensual, naked love. No longer frozen, I am totally surrendered, receptive. They seemed to be saying, *We are a part of each other. We are with you. We love you.*

Whales are the yoga of the sea, moving and breathing with strength, stretching into the universe, the yoga of divine connection. Their movements encourage—no, actually require my body to mirror them. As the whales reach their flippers and tails towards the sky I find my body stretching, releasing the knots that have been held so tightly. The rolling motion of the whales' 50-ton bodies opens my chest to fluidity and a sense of freedom. As their heads rear up for breath, I too elongate my neck and throat and breathe. Breaching, soaring towards the sky, flying through the air and landing in an enormous, volcanic splash in the sea, is an explosion of joy and exuberance that brings exclamations of awe from my lips.

Perhaps the most exquisite, in their movement of power and grace, is the tail stand, *cola*. Tailing for as long as twenty minutes, stretching the tail upwards, the whale's power radiates through my body, insisting that any slumps of defeat or despair are unnecessary. Reaching, reaching downwards toward the bottom of the sea and upwards toward the sky, the whale knows the connection of both, and my body responds.

As my body unconsciously mimics the movements of the whales, the connection becomes vast, powerful, and strong. So how then, in this world I live in, can I say the whales are my yoga teachers? Yet they are. They are yoga of sound, yoga of breath, yoga of sacred union, and yoga of the body.

My body responds and knows. It feels the sacred power and strength, it feels the blessed release of kinks and tightness, actually popping as it lets go. What beautiful teachers and what a beautiful body I have when I stop telling, forcing, attempting to control, and instead allow it to respond to the teachings of Creation.

The body carries wisdom and longs for freedom. It has held memories of forced captivity for far too long. Amazing joy erupts when given the freedom to respond. My movements are subtle and internal for the most part, possibly no one else on the boat even notices, yet they feel as vast as the universe. My beautiful teachers once again bring tears to my eyes, strength and flowing energy to my body, and connection to Creation.

CHAPTER 16

Union

§

Out beyond ideas of wrongdoing and rightdoing,
there is a field. I'll meet you there.

When the soul lies down in the grass,
the world is too full to talk about.
Ideas, language, even the phrase *each other*
doesn't make any sense.

—RUMI[25]

GREETED, WELCOMED, SEEN BY THE whales, my response was softening fluidity. The whales circled, diving underneath the boat, their energy, their spell weaving around and through us, as we became part of them and they part of us, moving together in a tapestry of love. Not even as separate strands weave but a merging, a dissolving of the strands to connection.

Although when one is first with the whales there is power, wonder, awe, and joy, there is still observer and observed. This then becomes a melting, shimmering union. It felt like what the mystics and sages call ONE. Blending so completely into the whale and the whale into me, I exploded into union with the sea and the sky, the land and the birds, with all. It is a powerful, deep truth. It is what Rumi wrote about so radiantly in the thirteenth century.

CHAPTER 17

The Song of the Whale

§

Sound is what our ancestors called 'the beginning.'
It is the *OM* of the East and the *Word* of the West.
It is the background noise of galaxies forming.

—DON CAMPBELL[26]

WHALES USE THEIR HAUNTING AND evocative song for communication and navigation. Their song also enchants and calls us. With sounds different from what we would normally call music, we are nevertheless spellbound by their unusual sounds and blows. Listening and listening, we hear the sound throughout our bodies, pulling us into a trance of awareness.

This use of vibrational sound has long been an aspect of sacred experiences. Drumming replicates the heartbeat, deepening consciousness into the heartbeat of the earth. In *When the Drummers Were Women*, Layne Redmond says of the early Roman church fathers, "Because they recognized its intimate connection with women's spiritual power, they banned the sacred frame drum."[27] Direct connection to Spirit is a threat to hierarchical control. Interesting. Perhaps it is now time to once again challenge control and hierarchy. Is this part of the call of the whales?

The expression of chanting also uses repetition and sound, changing brain waves and expanding consciousness. "The ancient art of chanting has long been embraced by the world's great religious traditions as a path to healing and enlightenment, but only recently has western science begun to recognize its therapeutic effects on the body and mind."[28]

So is this whale song, when heard or felt by humans, functioning as a drum, as a chant, cycling back, repeating and repeating, opening us to what the Native Americans call the Great Mystery, what we of the West would call God? Are the whales calling us in the ancient traditional way of sound, sending waves, vibrational waves, into the universe and into our souls? Much of the sounds and songs of the whale are of a frequency and at a depth that our ears are unable to register, but are our bodies responding, hearing in our own ways the call of the whale? Is it the call of Creation to open us to the sacred lessons we have long forgotten, lessons of direct connection, lessons of creativity, lessons of social justice, lessons of transformation?

When we consider all the uses technology has for sonar transmissions, we must conclude that natural sonar transmission will impact us. Possibly even releasing us beyond hierarchy and control.

CHAPTER 18

Becoming Present—
Consciousness and Whales

§

Creation . . . entices us as a lover does to a secret place
where it alone will play with us until we lose all sense of
past, present and future, and we become at last and in
spite of ourselves fully present to all space and all time.

—MATTHEW FOX[29]

THE RESONANCE IS IMMEDIATE. IT just feels good. I am often asked if
I am afraid in a small boat with such large whales. I was surprised the
first time I was asked this question because I have not been afraid. The
Southern Right Whales are huge, 50–55 feet long, bigger that the boat,
weighing approximately 50 tons. They swim under us and around us,
rising up so very close. But afraid, no. The resonance is so complete, so
embracing that the response is not fear, it is connection.

Being enveloped in the vibration and energy of whales unlocks a
capacity for total focus. We become completely here in absolute presence. Opened to a new frequency our consciousness expands. We open
to receive.

The sacred teaching of being here now in the present moment becomes a reality with the whales. Expanded and held, breathing with sacred breath, we shed the literal and enter into pure divine energy.

In his studies of consciousness and levels of vibrational energy, David Hawkins has studied the vibrational levels of sacred transmissions. He talks of the vibrational intensity and the attraction fields surrounding a teacher to pull the student into the field.[30] Could this then be the call of the whales? The radiating energy forms a field and we are taught. Our bodies respond to this energy, learning without words, shifting, expanding, transforming. The pull of a guru, just to be in the presence of sacred enlightenment, opens the possibility for transformation.

Roger Payne states that "The brains of whales suggest by their size and complexity a potential for function and/or thought equal to or surpassing our own."[31] Therefore, the energy of the whale would seem to be capable of this expansion of consciousness that Hawkins and others have researched. Not surprisingly this is something indigenous people have always known.

Energy and vibration have been used for centuries in many cultures, but we in the West are just now rediscovering the positive power of energy after using it for catastrophic destruction. There is currently an explosion in the study and use of energy medicine and vibrational healing. With the whales vibrating with an intensity that strongly connects to humans, the whales have a powerful potential role to play in healing us and opening our consciousness.

CHAPTER 19

The Lesson of the Seagull

§

Instead of limiting themselves to feeding on the loose
sloughing skin caused by sunburn, kelp gulls gouge out pieces
of live skin, creating crater-shaped wounds in the whales'
backs. Brown-hooded gulls don't do this, nor have kelp
gulls always done so. This behavior first appeared . . . in the
late 1970s . . . it is now a major source of harassment to the
whales . . . who writhe and twist to escape their tormentors.

—ROGER PAYNE[32]

CIRCLING THE WHALES, THE SEAGULLS swoop down and take a bite out
of the whale's flesh. I was told that at one time the shore became pol-
luted from the local industry so the seagulls could not eat their normal
diet. In order to survive they began pecking into the flesh of the whales.
The toxic dumping was stopped, the shore became clean again, and the
seagulls could return to the normal eating habits. Most did, but a group
of rogue seagulls did not. Generation after generation taught their off-
spring that in order to survive they must eat of the whale. They had
forgotten their natural way of living.

As I continue to experience my time in Argentina I realize that I too am a seagull. I have learned a way of living that I thought was necessary to survive. It is not who I am. I must return, like the seagulls must return, to a true essence. I am grateful to the seagulls for so visibly enacting the pain that is caused by living in a way that is not true, but a genetic distortion, a learned behavior that is harmful. I know that I cannot change or even understand my seagull ways on my own. I need the whales, the land and the sea, the wisdom of teachers, community and most of all the Creator's grace to be transformed.

I continue to be in awe and gratitude to the whales and the land for calling to me, for holding us with immense power and steadiness in the midst of all of our pain, and for showing us exquisite glimpses of joy and grandeur and love.

So this little seagull continues to flap her wings in prayer for Creation, for herself and for all of us, so that transformation can be.

CHAPTER 20

Why Can't You Just Let Us Love You?

§

Does compassion become the basic energy of the
universe? Surely this is what spiritual teachers East
and West have continuously taught: that the purpose
of living is to become the energy called love.

—MATTHEW FOX[33]

As WE SIT ON THE smooth rock cliff overlooking the sea and the whales, we four women pray our questions. We had not planned to come to the whales at this time, it did not fit into any of our practical agendas, yet we were pulled, so here we are. As I open I hear whales say, "Why can't you just let us love you?" The question is stated with love and puzzlement, not judgment. This is certainly not the guidance I expected from the whales, God, or Creation. I settle into the question, "Why can't you just let us love you?"

This may be one of the most profound spiritual lessons in my life. The quest, the measure of success, has been to do and to know, preferably in a factual and efficient way. Quickly accomplishing an array of activities, having answers to everything, and maintaining control have been the goal. This way of living has not brought wholeness or health for me or for the world. Could the whales' question, "Why can't you just let us love you?" perhaps be critical for us to hear? Creation nourishes, Creation embraces and loves, but we are too busy to see, hear, or feel. All the walls we erect in the name of safety because we are afraid we will not be loved, heard, seen, or understood cause enormous mistrust and misunderstanding.

But love is only a concept until it is felt. The natural world has been singing and dancing, blooming in a profuse riot of color, grace, and splendor. What would happen if we stopped and allowed the lushness of the natural world to permeate our separate, isolated, and cold human structures and ourselves? We could feel the love of a whale, or perhaps a tree, or a flower, or a bird. Stopping to feel the energy of love and beauty and joy, isn't that the communion that heals?

To be purely loved is so direct. All of the barricading clutter must be parted and removed so that the energy of love can penetrate. This clutter, this flotsam and jetsam, is so familiar. It defined who I am, who I thought I was. It consumed my time and energy. If it was removed, what would happen? Is this my resistance, my uncertainty?

Earlier in my opening to Creation it seemed impossible that the myriad of barricades could be removed. Now I know the blocks are dissolving and there is a choice involved. Will I continue to live as I have, controlled by pain, controlled by the actions of others, controlled by what society tells me I should do? Instead, can I act as I know, in creativity and truth, honoring the divine within myself as well as the divine in others?

To let the love flow, the pure love within me and others must be acknowledged and seen, respected and known. The explosion of inner love uniting with the outer love of Creation is birth. Ecstatic, open, pulsating connection. Creation knows this.

The piles and mounds of clutter—whatever form it takes for each of us—is the shell, the cocoon to be broken through, broken out of. The whales taught me this. The question, "Why can't you just let us love you?" Simple, so simple. Why not? Why not indeed.

Choosing to say "Yes" to Creation I stand and walk through the blockades to what is and has always been, creative love. It is the birthing call of the Universe.

CHAPTER 21

A Shamanic Initiation

§

The shamanic personality speaks and understands the
language of the various creatures of the earth. Not
only is the shamanic type emerging in our society, but
also the shamanic dimension of the psyche itself.

—THOMAS BERRY[34]

I ARRIVED IN PIRAMIDES WITH a friend and colleague. It was her first
visit to the whales in Patagonia. As we sat next to each other in the boat
eagerly awaiting the whales, a whale began swimming directly toward
us, raised herself up and blew a mist of water first on one of us, then
on the other. She did this over and over. We melted with joy, awe, and
wonder, feeling seen and feeling very, very welcomed.

Having been in Native American ceremonies together we felt it was
possible that the whale was greeting us with a shamanic initiation and
blessing. The spray glistened as it misted through the air and landed on
us. We loved it. It was a very strong experience and a very strong smell,
awakening us dramatically.

Shamans pray in ways very different from the Western world. They call
on the directions and animal spirits for wisdom and help. Becoming the

animals, the stones, the trees, and the mountains in deep communion they learn the ways of Creation. People in the West often say, "I don't need help, I can do it myself." Asking animals to teach me, learning from them how to live? No, a calm, quiet church of words is what should be. But as Thomas Berry says in the opening quotation, the way of the shaman is emerging.

In a workshop with Dorothy Maclean, one of the co-founders of Findhorn, we talked of doorways, gates into mystical, sacred connection to open communication with Creation. She spoke of divine intelligence waiting, waiting for humans to become partners, friends, collaborators in life. A doorway has been created by the whales. It is a doorway to another space, another time, another reality. They are waiting for us.

Blessed and seen by the whales, entering into direct communion and vibrational union, a language emerges. As the shamans learned from Creation, it is time for us to do the same. The whales are nurturing and loving us, giving us messages and wisdom. This goes way beyond anything linear, yet it is true for many of us. Divine intelligence is breaking through, if only we will listen.

Leaving control and narrowness of thought behind, we venture into the world of the whales. Expanding the literal definition of language, we can look at the tail that caresses the blind children, the blow that initiates and blesses, and the piercing eye that both embraces and challenges. Are these not communications?

Is it possible that the whales do interact with humans and form conversations? Titles of books like Alexandra Morton's *Listening to Whales* and Jim Nollman's *The Man Who Talks With the Whales,* the shamans, as well as the indigenous people who had a designated whale caller, seem to suggest the possibility. Many of us agree.

At the end of the powerful book and movie *The Whale Rider,* Kahu, the young Maori girl who validates the feminine and the whale, says to her grandfather, "Oh, Paka, can't you hear them? I've been listening to them for ages now. Oh, Paka, and the whales are still singing."[35]

Yes, the whales are still singing. Will we listen to what they have to say?

CHAPTER 22

The Science Teacher— Whales and Education

§

Facts by themselves are not enough,
what is needed is embodiment.

—BRIAN SWIMME[36]

THE CHILDREN SCAMPERED ONTO THE boat. It would be an afternoon with the whales. They had been studying them and had much information. Two teachers were with the children. One had been bringing her classes to the whales for fourteen years. She knew and loved the whales deeply. Her colleague was a scientist who had researched whales and had given the classes of students facts and figures.

As the whales came near the boat the science teacher began to cry and, in fact, tears filled her eyes through most of the outing. She was embarrassed to have this display of feeling in front of her students. The teacher who had been bringing students for years smiled quietly as she told us, "You know this science teacher has never been with a whale before. This is her first time." She had all of the information to teach academically but she had never experienced a whale. It was a wonderful lesson in head knowledge versus heart knowledge. How limiting knowing only through the mind can be. When the body is involved, all of the senses become involved, widening and deepening the experience.

How often we think we know and understand from words without the fullness of experiencing. As the mind quiets, the body comes alive. It is in this place of experience that I believe God truly communicates. It is here that healing and transformation can occur.

How beautiful for the children to see their academic teacher touched so deeply that tears came. There was a communion of feeling, of emotions, of knowing that we all—children, adults and teachers—were in the presence of something magnificent.

This is one of the lessons the whales teach. Come, come be with Creation. Don't just think about it, read about it, research it, and think you can teach it. Creation/Spirit is alive and must be lived, breathed, seen, felt, and experienced. What an arid life we live without the fullness of experience. The power of the whale steps through the masks and armor we put up to protect ourselves against pain, feelings, or even a call. The whales gently move through us, seeing us, embracing us, opening our eyes.

What if we lived all of our moments this way? Not just knowing facts but being alive, connected, part of all of life. This is the possibility the whales give. Once experienced, it is impossible to return to the caged life of only facts and information. The body and soul cannot be satisfied unless allowed to dance with Creation.

CHAPTER 23

Whales, The Hospital, and Western Medicine

§

But in our time we have virtually disowned the
"being" therapies. We refer to them pejoratively as
"placebo effects" implying that they are somehow
unreal. And whenever possible we have replaced them
with "doing" therapies such as drugs or surgery.

—Larry Dossey[37]

MY MOTHER BROKE HER HIP. Unable to think, remember, or communicate as she once could, the hospital was an unknown place for her,
filled with fear and confusion. In many ways I was a whale for my mom
during her months in the hospital and nursing home. Walking through
my own fear and discomfort in Western medical facilities, I prayed,
asking for help for my mom. I was told I knew what to do. Not what
I expected to hear from my prayer, but I realized I did know. Stepping
once again outside the boundaries of the absolute propriety, I created a
sacred space in the medical facilities. Just as the whales know it is not
human language, but presence and vibration that bring expansion and

potential healing, I sat with my mom in stillness, simply breathing. I brought music. The vibrational sounds of South American reiki music, Gregorian chant, and Shaina Noll's song, "How could anyone ever tell you, you are anything less than beautiful?"[38] not only calmed my mom, it astounded the nurses. One nurse said she felt like she was walking into a cathedral and another even called from her home as we were checking out to ask for the title of one of the CDs. We are so hungry for sacred space and presence. How sad that this is not practiced and understood in Western healing facilities more often.

I was able to walk with my mom through a very confused and difficult time, bringing steady, expansive, embracing love and vibration. I learned this from the whales.

CHAPTER 24

Global Politics and Prayer with the Whales

§

If we are interested in reducing the threat of terrorism,
what about a strategy of global good will that could make
us a beloved and respected nation, as we once were?

—BILL GRACE[39]

MY SECOND TRIP TO THE whales was two weeks after September 11th, 2001. Would I go? Should I get on a plane for international travel? Realizing that the work done with the whales is prayer, global prayer, prayer with all of Creation, it became clear that this was a critical time to pray with people from around the world. I would go. So I boarded the plane and flew to the whales in South America.

Then the U.S. began dropping bombs on Afghanistan. The international community was angry and horrified. We went out to the sea to pray with a Native American Pipe Ceremony. The sea captain announced that the bombing had begun and that a Native American shaman would pray with us.

So men, women, children, lovers, and families from all over the world, most who had never prayed in a Native Pipe Ceremony, prayed. Calling the directions, offering tobacco and song, we passed the tobacco around praying for wisdom for the leaders and for those who surely would lose their lives, we prayed for peace. As the ceremony was concluding, a group on the bow of the boat from Finland asked if they could also sing. In the middle of the sea, with the whales, dolphins, and seals around us, an a cappella choir sang *Alleluia*. It was a time of pain and a time of awe.

When I returned home I watched a video that had been taken during the ceremony. We did not realize it at the time, but 200 yards out the whales, dolphins, seals, and seagulls formed a circle around the boat during the ceremony. No one can watch the video without wonder and tears. Linear, rational . . . no, but absolutely real. We *all* prayed together. We are one. *Mitakuye Oyasin.*

CHAPTER 25

Return to the Crescent Beach

§

Assuredly, I say to you, unless you are converted
and become as little children, you will by no
means enter the kingdom of heaven.

MATTHEW 18:3

WE RETURNED TO THE CRESCENT beach and the baby came, a whale calf so alive, innocent, plucky, and curious, thrusting his small head out of the water—learning, looking, and breathing. The tenderness, the newness, the dignity of innocent purity touched my heart profoundly. New birth, a baby, the culmination of the trip and a beginning for me.

I walked on the crescent beach to say my goodbye when a small calf appeared. Could this be the calf born to the pregnant whale I saw on this same shore when I first arrived a week ago? The mother was clearly bringing her baby close so that we could see. Feelings of protectiveness surged through me, for the whale, for myself, for us all as we are birthed into a new world. Can we be in curiosity and innocence as this calf is, protected and guided by the Great Mother of Creation? Not letting our curiosity be stifled or shut down, allowing our innocence to remain, unafraid and in awe, knowing there is protection and wisdom embracing and guiding us? Can we? Our world needs us to do so. We are called by Creation.

CHAPTER 26

An Ancient Ceremony with the Moon and the Whales

§

The real work of religion is permanent astonishment.

I mean: blazing in blind ecstasy, drowned
in God and drunk on Love.

—RUMI[40]

A WILD FORCEFUL WIND WAS blowing, crashing the waves onto the beach. The port was closed. The sea was a blanket of white caps. The people of Argentina don't say "white caps," they say "lambs." There are too many lambs to be out in a boat. Powerful majestic Creation was giving a clear message that humankind is not in control. We are immersed and enveloped in something enormous, yet there is a choice. We can choose to shake our fists against nature that has the audacity to alter our plans or we can join with the power, the unpredictability, allowing the excitement and adventure to lead. Fighting against, trying to control Creation is a fight that cannot be won. It can only lead to anger and frustration. Joining, flowing with Creation leads to unexpected gifts.

So the adventure continued to unfold, as it always seems to with the whales. Unable to go out in a boat we drove to a beach that was more protected. The expanse of beach forms a crescent and we walked on the shore with the whales playing, splashing, and blowing. Sitting down on the pebble beach we wrapped ourselves in the large blankets we had each brought. Something ancient was beginning.

We were four women sitting on the red rock shore that stretched for miles and miles and miles without other humans or human structures. It was the vastness of the land meeting the vastness of the sea, and we four sat watching the whales play. A grandmother, a mother, a child, and I—generations of women blessing and being blessed by the sea as the wind blew.

We eventually decided to leave and then the ceremony began. As we four climbed into the car a whale came directly toward us. The young mother and I looked at each other, jumped out of the car, took our blankets to wrap around us, and walked to the water's edge to meet with the whale. As we stood wrapped in blankets, they became sacred coverings, the mother's dark blue with gold stars and moons, mine a lighthouse, sky and the sea in red and blue. A brilliant light appeared in front of us on the horizon. In silence we watched as the light became the orange ball of a full moon rising out of the water—huge, glorious, shimmering on the sea. The light formed a pathway that flowed through the water to the whale. Two more whales came, the three of them forming a circle directly in front of us, a circle of wholeness, joy, and connection in the moon's path. As we turned to see the grandmother and child in the car behind us, sheltered from the wind on a grassy dune, the sky behind them exploded into a sunset of fire. The full moon, the moon's path, the three circling whales, the two women robed in blankets, the grandmother and child and the radiant sunset were in direct alignment. A straight line of unexpected radiant power and beauty etched in eternity, connecting in aliveness and reverence. Creation's breath.

The port was closed. Responding to the call of a whale, the ceremony unfolded before our eyes. We were invited to join in the ritual. The physical response of glorious awe and gratitude remains.

We drove back to our rooms overlooking the gulf and stood in the darkness with the moon and the stars glistening. The waves crashed with the wind, lapping almost inside our windows as the tide reached its height. Once again we were bathed in Creation as Her fingers touched us with Her power.

CHAPTER 27

Infinity

§

According to the *Jaiminiya Upanishad Brahmana* (I, 5, 5; I, 35,
7–9; IV, 15, 2–5), the gate of the world of heavenly
Light is to be found "where Sky and Earth embrace."

—MIRCEA ELIADE[41]

THE SEA STRETCHED OUTWARD, SUMMONING my body to the edge of
the horizon where the tail of a whale reached up to the sky. The im-
mensity of the blue sky reached down to connect with the sea and the
whale. I was pulled to the edge. The whale's tail beckoned me. The sight
of an edge where the sea and the sky and the tail appeared seemed real;
surely if I went there, I would drop into the abyss. It was so far out. Why
would I be called out so far?

It must be more important to stay close, to deal with what is occur-
ring in my immediate vicinity. Why am I being pulled so far out? It is a
struggle and a quandary. Shouldn't I be taking care of what is near me?
There is so much going on. So many are in pain, confusion, and need
close by. Why was I called to Argentina and the whales and then called
outward, called to the edge where the sky meets the sea?

I allowed myself to release my tight hold on the known and float to what I had thought was the edge. I discovered something much different. The word "edge" transforms into forever, an experience of eternity and infinity. This became an understanding of the limited nature of my own strength and wisdom and the glory of connection with the universe. This stretch expanded the limited, rational, hard work that I perceived was always being asked of me. Stretched out, open to the expansion of the sacred universe, the edge is released. I am connected. We all are. The edge isn't. Forever is.

I returned changed, knowing that the vastness of the connection teaches. The wisdom will come. It is bigger. It sees a pattern, a necessity of experiences, of happenings to bring about growth for what is being called for. It is something I cannot do on my own. Breath slowed and deepened, just like whale breath. The whale had beckoned and I came, once again taught by the whales and the universe.

CHAPTER 28

Mating and Birth

§

We must simply be what we are, opening into a larger life.
Interior articulation of its own reality is the immediate
responsibility of every being. Every being has its own
interior, its self, its mystery, its numinous aspect.

—Thomas Berry[42]

THE WHALES CAME. TWO, NEXT to each other straight to me. They glided through the water with purpose and then they disappeared into the depths of the sea. As I looked out on the surface of the water two came again, directly, unerringly toward me, and then once again entered the depths of the sea. They left me shaken, exposed, and penetrated by their power, their focus and determination. This direct penetration continued and continued. The rhythmic circle became the lines of a poem or a song, gently, insistently, coming, coming into me.

It was the courting time of the whales. I too felt courted, mated, my body responding. The insistent repetition brought my body alive with ecstatic golden energy. And then a third whale appeared to join the other two. This is a dance of something bigger that my literal mind can analyze and grasp. Was this to bring forth a birth? Yes. As I stood in awe, I knew that what I am called to bring forth into the world is now purer, more essential, not the formula of success that I had been given by society. I am no longer following that formula, those rules. They have been shed, just like the elephant seal I stood beside after she shed her skin so that she could grow.

The land, the sea, moon, stars, and sun of Patagonia created a sacred container for the whales and for Creation to penetrate my soul. I gradually released what I no longer need to hold onto. Like "Jonah's incubation and rebirth from the 'womb' of the whale"[43] the whales have incubated me in their womb for rebirth. I am becoming free to dance in the universe. I twirl again on the beach, electric with joy.

In the midst of the whales, dolphins, penguins, elephant seals, seagulls, and cormorants, connected to people from all over the globe, I am now a woman living in Creation's world, not limited by one country, one race, or one religion. All is. The whales called me and taught me. Creation is my university. I breathe with the cosmos in gratitude and awe. New and still vulnerable in my newness, I surrender, changed forever by the whales in Patagonia.

Where will this new birth lead? I have shed my good girl and with strength and certainty said "No" to falseness, instead demanding integrity. I speak out for truth and authenticity, no longer caring what people might think. The awe, moving through the darkness, moving into creativity does bring the strength to act for social justice. Not living on the sidelines but in the midst of life.

It has been mainly women who have come to the whales. The women are learning to see, to stand up, to speak out. As I look at the world and the chaos of pain caused by the perversion of the authentic masculine, I see a gaping hole where the strong authentic feminine is also absent—too quiet, too afraid, and too numb. I see myself and the other women who have been asleep and compliant, not allowing ourselves to see the options our souls have been crying for.

Gathered together with the whales, we women and a few brave men began to uncover what we have always known. We become free as we are seen by Creation, seeing and respecting ourselves, our unique selves as an offering to the universe. We joined in circles encompassing people from all over the world, holding each other as Creation and the whales hold us. We need each other. Speaking out for love, for connection, for joy, respect, and social justice; honoring this precious earth, we become beacons for a world that can no longer function with power, money, control, and fear as our god. We see something bigger and more beautiful and creative. The time has come. Creation and the whales have called us. We are being seen, loved, and made loved to so that birth will occur.

CHAPTER 29

The Eye

§

We receive a brief flash of communion, of unified
thought and feeling, and we escape the bounds of our
regular life. The experience of that first penetrating
look into the eye of a dolphin or a whale creates an
explosive expanse inside the human mind. One feels
that a portal has just opened up in space and time. A
pathway to another being, one who understands.

—SCOTT TAYLOR[44]

A GENTLE RAIN FELL ON the calm gray sea. The first calm in six days and it beckoned us to come. We were ecstatically excited. We had been waiting and it seemed as if the whales had been waiting too. There were six of us—the sea captain, a photographer, a psychodramatist/physician, a biologist, a local whale lover, and me. Two men and four women entered the sea in a small zodiac that intimately cradled us in the water.

Is it possible to fall in love with a boat? Like so much of this adventure my love affair with an object was a surprise. My boat love was a zodiac, small intimate, and welcoming. A thin membrane of skin that just barely separated me from the sea, the whales, the dolphins, and the seals. The low sides were only a whisper of a barrier. With wide smiles we became one with the undulating sea, her creatures, and our divine interior. The zodiac, the vehicle that welcomed us on the voyage of transformation, material object that she is, became alive in her purpose, taking us through gateway after gateway to the awe of Creation.

The whales began to come and we entered the dreamtime of the whales and the sea, deeper and deeper as the soft mist anointed us. We were alone in the gulf, encircled by the natural pyramids of the Peninsula Valdes.

The whales came, closer, closer, circling and seeing, more powerful, more embracing than ever. They reared up to see us, curious. There was a joyous *hola*, hello, the loving excitement of reunion. Deeper and deeper we went into their time and their world. As they circled and swam under the zodiac, one whale brought her flipper to the upper edge of the boat caressing the length of the boat and us. Hearts opened to Creation. The caress was returned when the whale again came close by the boat and the beautiful young biologist glided her fingers over the whale in gentle love.

With my body opened in trust, blending with the group, the zodiac, the sea, and the whales, I drifted, floating in the warmth of communion. A whale rolled on her side, her eye gazing at me in steady penetration, capturing my body, my essence, in a laser connection radiating the cells of my body with insistence. This was not a casual glance. It was a challenge. A challenge to who I am. It was not a request, it was much too strong to have the aspect of asking that a request has. It was not a demand with the overpowering aspect a demand often has. It was purer than either. The eye seemed to be saying, "OK. Are you going to step up to the plate? You are ready? You are needed. So, what is your answer?" I joined a new race, a sisterhood/brotherhood this day.

As the zodiac continued floating, a whale came to the stern of the boat, positioned herself directly in front of the captain. She soared upward, stretching out her flippers in a huge embrace and blows, cascading a spray of water, drenching the captain's entire body in a baptism. We stood in awe, as did he. Although many of us have been sprayed by the whales, this was an embrace and an astounding showering cascade of water. He is a man who understands, loves, and respects the whales. He is indeed a blessing to the sea, to the whales, and to those of us who are with him in his boat. The whales seem to agree and they are telling him.

We became Meister Eckhart's words, "The eye with which I see God is the same eye with which God sees me."[45] We were in communal ecstasy, vibrating with awe and joy. We were dancing together, joined, connected, in silence, reverence, song, tears, and laughter. We shared mate, the traditional South American drink of community, ceremony, and communion, surrounded by the whales in the middle of the sea.

Returning to my room, I walked into my bathroom and the light that radiated from me bouncing off the mirror startled me so much that I jumped out of the room into the hallway and then cautiously returned to the mirror to look. White light, so strong and bright that I could hardly keep my eyes open. Blessed indeed!

We gathered for conversation and tea, settling on big puffy chairs and a sofa in the central area of the inn, looking out through the floor-to-ceiling windows to the sea, by now dark sky and stars. We were deeply touched and shaken, filled with excitement, awe, and joy. The desire to share the experience was strong. Whales have a communal impact.

Wanting to talk, yet stumbling over words we were unable to really communicate our ecstasy. The biologist says, "How can we possibly put this into words?" and we all laugh knowing that I was attempting to do that.

Words are so inadequate and pale in expressing the power and beauty we experience. Going so far beyond speech, the vibrating energy simply danced and played. And yet the challenge to speak was there, even with continued stumbling. Knowing how inadequate words were, I was being asked to express the profound, glorious experience of Creation and God's love through the whales in Patagonia.

CHAPTER 30

Becoming the Whale—A Healing School With the Whales

§

The cleanest bones serve *Wakan-Tanka* and
the Helpers the best, and medicine and holy
people work the hardest to become clean.

—FOOLS CROW[46]

Psychodrama is the seminal action
method of experiential therapy.

—ZERKA MORENO[47]

AS WE GATHER TOGETHER TO spend time with the whales, it has been in
relatively small groups with some who are returning and some who are
coming for the first time. I approach each visit with enormous anticipa-
tion and stay with the whales for many days. The teachings are different
each time and they are cumulative. Our experiences and encounters are
unique and individual, yet a theme often arises. It is as if the seminar
topic is chosen by Creation and we each discover our part of the whole.

In the group we will become the whales to more deeply understand what we are learning. The sea, the whales, the ancient land, and the sky become the container for sacred psychodrama, theater of the soul to emerge.

We say yes to a time with the whales, answering the difficult, exciting, and necessary call to heal ourselves so that the love of Creation can flow through us in the world, with both strength and radiance. The awe, joy, and tenderness of witnessing this cleansing and letting go is an experience of profound honor.

As we shed our coverings, the whales do indeed speak. We hear powerful knowings from these whale beings, telling us again and again that we are seen and loved. We are shown how to play with joy and wild abandon. We are asked to stand up, speak out, and walk our path.

As our bodies reenact our experiences, these knowings become integrated and profoundly understood. We are witnesses for each other. Intimacy flows, the threads weaving a container of support and love. As people step forward to share their whale teachings and are willing to clear what has been stopping them, all of us are lifted into a place of hope. Working together, we see each other, just as the whales have seen us. Radiance bursts forth. Connecting to Creation and each other, we are birthed, transformed, and given courage to take the next step in our creative unfolding. We watch each other in sacred awe.

We begin to more deeply understand that we are born unique, precious beings of God to be nurtured and brought forth in our divine selves. The need for approval, for control, the apology for existence, and the fearfulness of not being right can no longer be driving forces in our lives. The whale wisdom, challenge, and love connect with the circle of whale lovers and breathers, calling us to be, in this world that needs our strong, unique divine selves. This becomes the birthed self of creativity, transformation, and love.

The threads hold, the whales remember us, we form a global connection. In a world separated by nationalism, fundamentalism, and ruthless power we know there is something so much more than that limited vision. We are people who come from the far ends of the globe, respecting and listening to each other, respecting and listening to Creation. As we transform, the transformation radiates outward to our families, friends, workplaces, and communities. Sacred yarn weaves a world that can be joy, beauty, justice, peace, and love, becoming a global dance as we listen to Creation and the call of the whales.

As the cry of my soul is heard, I say a prayer of immense gratitude to Creation. Instead of being coaxed into anti-depressant medication so that I could fit into the world as it is, I was led to South America and the whales to discover what the world could become. What an enormous relief—to be loved and belong to something so much more beautiful, creative, and blazingly brilliant than the literal, commercial, material world of economic power and consumption.

I was vaulted into a world of Creation that offers joy and adventure, hope, possibility, creativity, compassion, strength, and purpose. It is a spiral circle of grace that leads to transformation. My longing for wholeness and for God was heard. I have been held in a circle of love by Creation and the other courageous souls who have taken this trek with me. My gratitude is infinite. I have been in a healing school with the whales, a university of the sea. I did not have to stay in the cage, the jail, the box. I have been freed by Creation.

CHAPTER 31

The Call—Embracing and Embraced by Creation

§

Let who you are ring out and resonate
in every word and every deed.
Yes, become who you are.
There's no sidestepping your own being
or your own responsibility.

You are the message.

—LEONARD PELTIER[48]

WHAT IS THIS CALL TO the whales? It is so strong that for some of us it cannot be ignored. From my first "Yes" to an invitation to the whales, the call, the link has intensified. Dismissing practicality, the song of the whale flows through me and I continue to board the plane for the long journey from Seattle to Patagonia. It is a belonging, a love affair, an opening to sacred wisdom. I know I must continue to go.

Where is this taking me? I do not know for certain. Yet I know that I am walking a path, a very ancient path that many have walked before me. It is a path of respect and reverence, a path of openness and willingness to learn, a path that is the true meaning of prayer, which is love.

Again and again I am enraptured and in love, a woman in love with the whales, the land and the sea of Patagonia, opened to the love of Creation. As I write these words in a log cabin in the San Juan Islands of the Pacific Northwest, five eagles suddenly fly overhead. Creation speaks.

What a tender treasure this Earth is, holding us in Her nurturing embrace.

Can we learn to hold Her and all of Her inhabitants in this same embrace, loving and being loved by the magnificence of Creation?

This is the call. We are the message.

In the Presence of Grace

§

THE FOLLOWING PHOTOGRAPHS EXQUISITELY DOCUMENT the luminous beauty, power, and blessing of being embraced by Creation and the Southern Right Whales.

The photographs were taken in the waters of the Peninsula Valdes, Argentina, by Angel Velez in 2004 and 2005. Reprinted by permission.

Fig. 1. The ancient cliffs of the Peninsula Valdes, Argentina

Fig. 2. Anticipation

Fig. 3. The whale approaches

Fig. 4. Meeting the whale

Fig. 5. A mating group

Fig. 6. Mother and calf and seagull

Fig. 7. A mother nursing her calf

Fig. 8. The blow

Fig. 9. Breaching

Fig. 10. A whale tailing in the sunset

PART TWO

Other Voices

If a man does not keep pace with his companions,
perhaps it is because he hears a different drummer.
Let him step to the music which he hears,
however measured or far away.

—Henry David Thoreau[49]

Whale Lovers

The following pages are the radiant writings and interviews of people from the U.S. and Argentina who have been with the whales in Patagonia. I am enormously grateful and honored that they are willing to share their soul journeys and their experiences with the whales.

Thoughts on Whales
By A U.S. Businessman

§

I'M NOT SURE I CAN really write my thoughts about the whales in Patagonia and have the words convey their real impact, but here goes.

I believe that everyone's experience in really visiting the whales seems unique and different but that is because the experience is filtered through the unique life history we each bring. The underlying message is the same.

My own background includes significant success in athletics and academics in high school and college and a very extensive business consulting career where I had the opportunity to work with many major companies, governmental organizations, and universities.

For me the experience of the whales is much broader than the impressive visual impact of these huge mammals. I wonder why they choose the bays of the Peninsula Valdes to visit. Sure, the bays are shallow and provide some natural protection from killer whales, but I also think they choose this location for other reasons. The Native Americans believed that the whales carry the history of the world. It seems to me that there may be many places that would also provide the same protection from predators, but few that provide the sense of history that one sees in this location.

The whales seem to have an understanding of this world and its place in the universe that we humans seldom grasp. They preceded us as a life form on this planet and will probably succeed us as well—if we do not exterminate them. I think the whales choose the Peninsula Valdes because of its visible history of millions of years of evolution of this planet in the rocks and cliffs of this area. This setting provides an ideal environment for their message.

When I first visited the whales they talked to me. I had waded into knee deep water in the bay and heard their variable tones clearly. The sound was not audible when I left the water but was very clear when I returned. Since that time I have gradually begun to understand their message and my perspective of life has significantly changed.

For me the whales bring a message of how precious and important all life is. They provide a connection to the divine by contacting me in an environment that clearly illustrates millions of years of history on this planet and demonstrates how fragile and wondrous each part of life is. They cause me to focus on the wonders of life on earth and challenge me to pay attention to all aspects of it. They have led me to many new and interesting friendships that I never imagined. They have helped me to place less emphasis on the material and power messages that constantly bombard me in this society and to focus more on the value of all life, especially on connections with loved ones and with others who search for the guidance of the divine.

Not everyone has the chance to experience the whales, but when you have heard them speak or been touched by one or looked one in the eye you are forever changed.

CHAPTER 34

Letting Go—Releasing with the Whales

By A Health Educator

§

MY EXPERIENCE WITH THE WHALES was both more subtle and more dramatic than I expected. It was rather windy and rocky all of the times we went out on the boat. Although we were in the fresh air and I had never felt seasick on a boat in my life, the first trip out to see the whales was two hours of nausea for me. My friends were reminding me to breathe, pointing out the beauty of the whales, and I was trying to pay attention, but my own feelings of sickness were distracting. The whales were gentle and beautiful, but I found that it helped more to focus on the land, which I could only see intermittently as the boat rocked between land and sea.

The second time I thought I might feel better, and I did. Although it was still rocky, I hoped that perhaps I had gained my "sea legs" and would be prepared for the magnificent experience that everyone had talked about. A pair of whales circled the boat. It's amazing how close they get. I had been feeling better than the last time, but then suddenly realized I was going to throw up. I never throw up. How embarrassing—it's messy and everyone would know. But maybe I had been holding too much in for too long. Now that I was among nature and supportive people, and I was in a completely different hemisphere, it was okay to let go. As soon as I was done, a whale changed its course and headed straight for me. It was reassuring and comforting to me. From it I got the message that it's okay to fall apart, it's okay to be vulnerable. In fact, that may be essential to my growth as a person.

The whale saw me. I realized that I needed to both see myself and to make sure other people see me. That I need to stand up for myself and my needs, even if it is uncomfortable or unpopular. I had been trying to keep other people happy and forgetting about myself as an equal player. I think this is a pattern that many women fall into, and it needs to stop. We need to support each other in speaking out, acting out, whatever it takes to help us feel fulfilled in life and make our presence known in the world. Now that I am home and have decided to quit my toxic conference planning job to find something more fulfilling, the messages of the whales stay with me and give me strength.

CHAPTER 35

Essential Purity—A Gift
of the Whales
By An Artist

§

THERE ARE MANY WORDS TO describe the whales—elegant, graceful, free . . . but after I saw them for the first time up close, I have to use the words *essential* and *pure*.

Like my experience with the landscape—the raw barren cliffs—when watching the whales I felt that everything that did not matter was stripped away, and what was really real and enduring, remained. The things the world tells you are important—material success and accomplishment, power over others, the ability to do five things at once—these things had no place here.

In Piramides, I felt like the universe rose up to meet me, to tell me what really mattered. A sense of mystery, a spiritual connection with nature, a deeper understanding of oneself—these are the things that matter. These are the things that last. I was not alone in this land, in this world. The whales reminded me of this the first magical day we ventured out on the sparkling sea. The whales came up very close—spraying their fine mists at us, making noises, making us laugh. They reminded me to play and to know my connection. A female came up so close that I reached out my hand and she touched the tips of my outstretched fingers with the top of her head. I liked that she saw me, that she acknowledged me with her touch. She knew her place in the world and was encouraging me to know mine. What greater gift is there? This is essential. This is purity.

CHAPTER 36

Receiving from the Whales
By An Argentine Woman of the Sea

§

I'M SITTING IN MY ROOM, in front of the window, watching the sea. I'm listening to it because I have the windows opened, and it is incredibly nice. The sun is just coming down and it is full of whales blowing!

These days in Piramides I brought you with my mind and heart, and as I have promised you to write some experience that happened in this powerful and sacred place, now I'm ready to do it. Today is completely different from the days before because the sea and the wind are very strong. The past days the sea has been very calm and the whales showed much serenity.

We went out in the boat near noon, the sea was wavy and the captain decided to go far away to find more whales, even dolphins. We saw some whales with their babies but they didn't come to us. I was told that something was not OK with the group on board.

Suddenly I thought that we could pray to the Mother (*Virgen María*), holding hands all together and giving thanks to the sun, the sea, and the whales for embracing us. And we did so and it was very nice. Then we were asked to make a circle, and we tried one by one (not everybody could do it) to get in the middle of the circle to see how we felt there. And something very nice happened. A white baby whale showed up suddenly, then his mother appeared, and there was a great change with the energy. The whales started coming to the boat. One of them was playing with her tail, splashing the water. We also met a whale couple who were making love and they let us come near them.

So I thought that it is possible to make lovely things with good intentions. Also that it's different to be opened to receive whatever life brings. I am also discovering how the whales work with us so much and how the connection with them can repair the pain in our souls. It's wonderful, as you said before. This third time to me has been very special, very different from other times. I am very moved.

CHAPTER 37

Whales as Sacred Spirits
By An Argentine Man of the Mountains

§

I OWE YOU THIS MAIL since I'm back from Piramides, but I didn't want to write you until now, that I understand better what was that experience. I can tell you that I wasn't hooked to the experience until I did my first psychodrama, after it. Then I started to understand better what I was doing there.

I felt really that the whales were sacred spirits that can give us full strength, and I always remember you talking about them from the depth of your heart, telling that they spread energy all around them. And now I'm sure that is it.

I'm improving now in leaving bit by bit my anxiety about life and I'm sure I will do it. You know, I started to attend different courses and meditation and I'm doing with myself pretty well, always . . . step by step.

CHAPTER 38

The Whales and I
By A Patagonian Guide

§

MY EXPERIENCE WITH WHALES STARTED with dolphins first. I was living in Geneva (no seas in view) and yet the dolphins managed to come to me during a visualization Sophrology class to let me know that I should follow them. Then and there, the professor started talking about a "conscious conception" project that included going consciously through pregnancy and giving birth in the water, in the presence of wild dolphins. I was totally taken by this and I managed to fit in the project, not as a future mother, but as what now we could call a Doula. This took place following my studies of Psychology and Human Resources, and it was a splendid experience to apply all these concepts as a whole!

Ever since then, my whole life was led by the Cetaceans. My spiritual life was shown to me by them. Believe me, they have a very special way to make themselves understood, even if one is not near the water.

However, I used to carry their energy by having pictures of them all around me, as well as readings and all kinds of stuff. People have linked me with cetaceans ever since and I am sure it is not because of the pictures, but because of the real bond I have with them.

My first contact with them (whales and dolphins) was in Hawaii. I went whale watching in a fisherman's boat with my daughter, and when we saw them, we jumped in, just with our fins and snorkeling masks. We stayed there, in the middle of two islands, nothing above but the blue sky, nothing below but the blue sea, and the whales and us, in a beautiful ballet of the encounter of two species. They even sang for us, which was an incredible experience.

Many years later, I went back to Hawaii to visit my daughter again. She used to work in the Kewalo Basin Marine Mammal Laboratory, observing dolphin behavior to sign language. When the director found out I was Argentine, he asked me if I had ever gone whale watching there, since it was the best place in the world to have that experience. I admitted that I hadn't and I promised myself to do it as soon as I got the chance.

So after I got back, I decided to go in a matter of 24 hours. This was the time it took to think about going, ask a friend to come along, order the tickets, and leave! Everything went so smoothly and fluidly that it was unbelievable.

When we finally got to Piramides—a trip that we did with an incredible sense of urgency and a feeling of being "out of time and space"—the contact we had with the whales was overwhelming and all the expectations were totally surpassed. In fact, it was the month of May and we were the only passengers on the boat. Afterwards we found out these were the first whales that had been seen in the season! No wonder the hurry! Everything was synchronized!

Then, we wanted to share this experience and thus the idea to create the workshop started. Many have had extraordinary experiences with the whales during the workshops and their stays in Piramides. It is impossible not to!

And now, the last big happening is that I have *moved* to live by them, and I can enjoy their presence now every season, from June till December. I can communicate with them and consciously work together with them in the healing of the planet and of humankind.

CHAPTER 39

Becoming Free
By An Argentine Woman

§

THEY SAY THAT THE ONE that finds it, will no longer be the same.
Who drinks of its water changes her destiny.
One autumn morning she decided to make a decision . . .
To set out to meet herself.

One day in June she decided that the story was going to change. The indefatigable loneliness was her shadow, that loneliness of oneself, lack of INHABITING oneself—

Empty
Alone
Dark

There she went . . . she ran hard and dared.
At home a family close to the breaking point, three children and a girl that howled, a tear in her soul and an emptiness of echo in her spirit.
She departed with her old bag to board the plane that would leave her in an ancestral land.
The South, the place where she had been invited to for the encounter.

She looked through the window of the plane and crystallized each tear in her eyes into wishes—sincere, deep, and filled with illusion. She smiled at the wonder of the sun and within she wondered, *Who am I?*

For an instant that girl rose and observed . . . who was that Woman truly and where was she going in such haste?

The small stretch of her life had convinced her that many things are not what they seem, but that there are some that RESEMBLE them so much. From one encounter to the other she wove her weave.

Ahead will be a chain of strong women that support her transformation, awaiting her emergence from her chrysalis.

Her soul floated in the midst of wise women anchored steadily to this land, firm and deep, fragile and sensitive. For all of them the wheel had turned just in time, thus receiving in each act their initiation.

The wheel or the circle of holiness happens. A person is born to the circle, it is then when everyone moves a place and the spiral adds a place in the cosmos. IT IS THE LUMINOUS EXPERIENCE of each being. To see it is to attend the most divine combination between God and human. Thus the daughter comes to be mother, and the mother grandmother, and the grandmother great-grandmother, and then a free and sensitive soul.

To float is the most sensitive and vital way of feeling oneself supported without making an effort.

Where to anchor?

With Courage she decided to go into the sea, and observe what happened. And it happened.

The whale's presence knocked her door and made her loose her self-control, let go of everything that she was holding to. She did not understand. She fell on the floor and after vomiting she slept.

She felt that something very dark had taken her soul. The structure had fallen and in the presence of the GREAT WOMAN floating in that water, she heard the WORDS "be free," and for the first time she was. That darkness began to transform into light and she decided. She let go of absolutely everything. She offered it and BECAME ALIVE.

It was magic. Each time the whale appeared she enjoyed the motherly encounter that the whale offered so lovingly. Desperate, she asked how to be free with so much fear? How? To that the whale did not answer; on the contrary, she submerged in her magical and profound world.

She felt that she could not govern her body, neither her fluids nor her air. It was all in chaos, and her soul was adrift . . . at sea.

She slept for a long time. Then in the company of a circle of women healers she TALKED.

In immaculate respect a breeze covered them and the turquoise color of the Sacred vibrated between them.

Once again with Courage she decided to go into the sea, and observe what happened, and it happened. The whale once again blew by her ear, stood up and gave her the possibility of opening the luminous channels, to allow for God's creation to manifest.

She fell in an ambush . . . which was the light in the midst of such darkness. Each time she locked herself in her dark weaving the whale submerged and left her.

She cried and cried in such despair.

She cried and looked towards the sky, asking God how to BE? How to rebuild? How to submerge in peace in this life filled with questions, loaded with moments of guilt and with the need for high wisdom.

The sun was setting, a group of dogs followed her, and she discovered that many of those women so firmly grounded to the land had asked loudly to open their channels to heal.

With much love she went back to the boat and discovered that she was not alone. "You are not alone."

At night she went back to the gulf and breathed together with the whale, both in rhythm and time—together.

It was there that she felt the wonder of being cradled in her mother's embrace. That sense of feeling the chest of your mother when she soothed you or made you sleep to the rhythm of her breathing.

To breathe together. She closed her eyes and let go. Holding to that great mother she let the circle turn.

AND IT TURNED.

When autumn declines your nature
Your light leaves
Your wilted flowers
Of firmness filled,
Concentrate the life yesterday held
And be nourishment for the new earth
With the rain they penetrate your layers
Searching for a light in the darkness
And the day has come
When that light begins to reign
From your center
Glowing with a strength more and more intense
Until lighting up the dark
Until reviving the dead
Until emerging to air
In which the soul breathes
To give it new breath.

Back on this land, I could arrive in a new and different way, with the live experience of feeling that one only keeps what one does not tie, and that I have the freedom to center in my soul each decision and possibility of light on my way.

I am water in my blood
I am air in my breath
I am earth in my body
I am fire in my soul.

To live tied to the past is a good way of not fearing the future, but to live the present is a good way to redeem our past road and to bless and thank our present. The whales know it. They have the information of an immense and inexhaustible ancestral past and they have the gift of transforming it into an immensely luminous present.

Everything is simple; there is not a law. EVERYTHING is transformed.

Maybe I feel that my mom had some resemblance to the whale, most certainly in her spirit, in the wisdom of the years and the patience and freedom for things to happen.

They say that since she came back, her life was not the same. The girl grew, was woman and mother.

Today I discover that intimate transformation is personal and particular to each being. On this path we all go and we are souls of transformation, facilitators for one another.

So in each act
one vivifies the vibration of her soul,
and in the vibration of each soul
is the mysterious melody of each being—
everyone,
and each one of us
that plays an instrument
make a part of the orchestra
and shares the symphony of life.

For Paula who knew it was the time, to Monica who knew to let me transform in the midst of so much pain, to Amy for choosing me in her psychodrama of the vomit (which allowed me to be aware), to Flo for her sensitivity, to Diane for the "cafes con leche" on the white couches, for her psychodramas at 4 A.M., and for her love, to Juan that made us sing in the lobby of the hotel, to Verity for her balancing, to Viva for being different, to the dogs that watched, and to Juli for celebrating Christmas with us.

And to the whales an immense gratitude for the chance they gave me to be. To Be.

To be a part of the weaving.

Interview with the Senior
Sea Captain in Piramides

§

WHEN DID YOU FIRST KNOW the whales?

It was 1971, I found my first whale while I was diving looking for octopuses. It showed up right in front of me! I was greatly surprised because at that time, whales did not stay here in the Gulf as they do now, that came later.

In 1972 I worked with Jacques Cousteau on the *Calypso*, and from the helicopter we did not see any mothers and calves; we only saw a little group feeding right in front of Piramides. There is a deeper area there, where some of them stir up the bottom of the sea to eat just enough for their southbound migration, a long distance trip indeed.

At the beginning of the '70s they would stay to give birth, court and mate mostly at the San Jose Gulf, however they were very, very few. This was the last year before the International Whaling Commission finally signed the international treaty to stop whale hunting, including Russia and Japan.

By then only four hundred and fifty whales could be located by the satellites; they were close to extinction. But after the whaling stopped, the population started to grow little by little. Nowadays there are more than a thousand who have been identified just in this area, and the total population is estimated to be three to four thousand. The area where they live is very widespread—South America, New Zealand, Australia, and Polynesia. I think the Northern Right Whale population has not increased as much, there are still just a few and humans should strive to help them out.

It is very nice for me, having lived with whales since they were almost extinct to be here when their numbers have recovered so much. I am very happy to see that.

Tell me more about the first time, when you were diving.

It was wonderfully close, I was catching octopuses with the hook, a long hook, and I felt something strange, a different movement in the water and went up to see a very big circle. "This is not a sea lion." They would come to take my octopuses away so we were always fighting. I was in apnea, without tanks. I put my snorkel-mask in the water and saw the eye! It was fantastic.

That was very moving. You can see only one eye, if you are high above the water you can see the callosities on them, but always you can only see one eye. It is a very clever eye, very intelligent. How they come to the boat and observe us, touch the boat, feed their calves, how they defend them as well, it all shows us behaviors that are very interesting and important in nature. How they move, they can do a circle in the same place, they are fantastic animals.

When the eye looked at you, did you think it was saying something to you?

No, mostly I believe it was wondering what is this strange animal doing here—me! I was the one invading her habitat, not the other way around.

So you don't think that whale came and said, this man may sometime be special for us?

No, I was the intromission in her water. I do not know, but I think that the animal was important for Me.

That is sometimes the difference with people. There is more ethic in the whale's life than we have. Man [*sic*] may live wherever, but we do everything for money. We can live in love/balance with nature but when money talks, differences and imbalance appear. This would be impossible in nature.

Whales have a lot of things that we have lost because they are of this Earth. We do not have their hearing, their orientation ability, their ability to move.

Why are the whales important, to you and to Creation?
They are angels, ancient beings. They have a perfect balance.

Do you think that if human beings spent more time with whales our ethics and morals would change?
Of course! Balance is one of the most important things. We can be rich because our forebears were the conquerors of this land, because they saved money through time, for a number of reasons. If we put balance in our minds and look towards nature, there are many things that would balance people. We are a lot of people but nature says to us, "Care for these." If you look, there will be resources for everyone, but not as a business, not for profit. Balance is very difficult now for humanity. I don't believe in any religion, the balance is for all. There are rights and obligations and then there are some that have too many rights.

When you came in contact with the whales or as you say other parts of nature, does that . . . ?
Whales are my biggest representation and I think they are very important. Nature keeps the balance.

Can people be changed and reach a place or an experience with whales when the whale's eye looks at you and says something?

It depends on how people interpret what they live. Whoever looks at nature's balance is looking at God. There are people that come here and talk—ecologists—who almost want to kill humanity! That is not the problem; it has to do with education programs, schools. How to live on Earth. We live in nature and we need to see how to develop our full potential here.

Give me a few sentences about whales, about you and about people that have been with whales.

Whales are the biggest animal in nature and are an expression of nature's power. It is the most important thing available for humans to learn about nature's importance. They are the Bible of Nature.

CHAPTER 41

Interview with a Current Sea Captain

§

Would you tell me how it was first with you with the whales?

It was always from the coast, I lived here in Puerto Madryn (town near Piramides). I was born here, so I'd go walking to school and see them. I didn't take it as something that was so special because I didn't know what they were.

I think that what happened to me is the same as what happens to all of those who have never gone whale watching. One thing is to see them where one lives and the whales come visiting, another thing is to go on the boat and share a moment with the whales. They are very different sensations; there is a change (difference).

Do you know why there is a difference?

When people say, "Let us go to Peninsula Valdes to see the whales," they say it in the same way that they would say, "Let us go see the sea lions or sea elephants." But when they spend a while with the whales, it changes. Unfortunately this special moment with whales is not always achieved. Some people may go away without realizing that they have *lived* a moment with the whales.

Sometimes without my realizing a connection is achieved, I realize once it has happened because we all have experienced a special something with the whales. If I look for it, it will be harder to find. So when I start an outing I never know which whale I will approach. I go out searching, not trying to find the closest whale but looking for 'The Whale.' Sometimes because of a fin showing or flapping, a tail or some special movement, I get closer and that is the one that was looking to make contact.

Do the whales call you or invite you?

It is usually me who is searching, looking for the one that will let me come closer. It is not always the closest and that is why, for me, it is very important that outings should last at least an hour and a half, not just for forty-five minutes or an hour. Because if you are pressed for time, if you have less than an hour, then you have to approach the closest whale and follow her, as if chasing her. I don't like to follow them or go after them if they are not willing. Then they should not be bothered.

I am ignorant of anything that is spiritual, but I do realize when there is a special moment. It is a feeling you perceive instantly, as if I'm saying something and I have this feeling that it was the whale that transmitted it to me without my realizing. It does not always happen, but I have had very powerful experiences.

Related to the question you asked before about if there is ever a rejection from the whales, what I am going to tell you is something that will describe it on its own.

I go out on the boat with three Frenchmen who came to make a documentary film and a park ranger. Of the three Frenchmen, two worked filming underwater. We go out and find a very sociable young male whale. I leave the two divers there and they stay for almost forty minutes, making as many pictures as they need, touching him and caressing him. The whale lets them film as much as they want. When they run out of air, they give me a call so as to change the film and fix the camera. Then the third Frenchman on the boat, desperate to swim with the whale, forcefully pulls the suit away from one of the divers and goes into the water. The whale had been waiting by the boat until that moment, but he goes away as soon as the man jumps in. I pull him on board and advise him not to hurry, to take it easy. Again, I get close to where the whale is. He jumps in and the whale goes away. Next time, as we get close to the whale, one of the first divers who was still wearing his suit goes into the water and the whale remains close. When this third man goes into the water, the whale moves away once more.

I believe it is impossible to recognize a person with all the diving gear, suit, goggles, and everything; specially taking into account that this man was wearing the same suit as one of the divers had been wearing while filming the whale. So it was not his outer appearance; this man transmitted something that the whale could perceive and made it go away. That was unbelievable—he could not get any closer than seven feet! As soon as the whale saw him, it moved away.

Whales take care of us all the time; they take care of us even from their own babies. Like that time we were at Pardelas and you were there, my son too. We had the propeller turned off watching a courting group of three whales, and there was a mother with her baby coming close. Suddenly the baby changed direction and came right towards the boat, touched us and bumped against the boat. It was blowing hard like upset, and two adults came and took him away with their pectoral fins.

You told us he was going to hit the boat and to move to the back.

I remember they had room to pass if they kept the same course as they had, but the baby saw something at the boat and came towards it.

It is a surety that adults and sub-adults protect us, do not want to do us any harm, otherwise with their jumps, tails—anything could happen. Mostly considering that not all of us captains have the same attitude towards whales. And that is a problem.

Before we continue, I want to say that when you used the words that you are ignorant of spirituality, I think that is not true. I think you are very wise. You know the real place of Spirit.

I used those words because I did not study it, I did not read it. If I feel it, it is not because I know it.

The feeling is the knowing; that is where we have gotten so crazy, thinking that everything has to do with words and dogma.

What about the children? How is it different or the same with the children?

There is a difference in the behavior on the boat, there are children's outings and there are retired people's outings. With the children it is easier to tell them not to yell, not to run on the boat, to try for a quiet outing, and it is easy to get them to follow these indications. They will move around from one side to the other but these outings are easier to keep under control than the elders' outings.

Sometimes you will tell the elders to keep the boat in balance and they just do not care. Once I talked with one of the elder passengers and asked him why he would not follow my indications and that it was dangerous for everyone to be on the same side of the boat. His answer was that they were already round the bend, "coming back," that they did not care anymore. (He uses an Argentine saying meaning that you know all that there is to be known.) So with that person in such a frame of mind it is very difficult to achieve a whale-person connection.

With special children, handicapped children, the connection is much easier. I will give you an example of an outing only for special kids with a different captain.

This was a nice, calm day, there were two blind girls with this group and a whale stayed close by, moving from one side of the boat to the other, quietly. After a while, it dived and its tail appeared right against the boat. Let us remember that a whale's tail can weigh up to 6,000 pounds. The tail showed up just where these two girls were and the whale curved and lowered it so that the girls could touch it. The tail was against the boat and the whale held steady in place. Then the current made the boat move so that the tail was going to bump against the rail, only when the tail touched the rail, the whale lifted it and smoothly followed the movement of the boat. They are incredible contacts.

Another captain, who was not very sensitive to whales, once took out a young handicapped man on a zodiac and the whale they were watching touched this young man with her fin. After the experience this captain acknowledged that the whale communicated with this man, but only that.

Many times diving with the whales, though not enough times, I touched them and caressed them, but in the last season something special happened.

I had turned off the propeller and this whale kept on taking its flukes out of the water right behind the boat, where the blades are, which is the most dangerous place for her. I stood on the back step and every time the boat moved away from her because of the wind she would dive and bring her flukes out again, right behind the boat, and every time the flukes came closer to the boat. So I started to touch her, since they will normally go away when you touch them, but she got even closer! I was standing on this step, the boat behind me and the flukes in front of me; I held this tail and kissed it. The sensation I had then was very different from the one I had touching it with my hands; this was a very pleasurable feeling, hard to describe, like a soft electric current in my face and lips. It was incredible! Every time you go out there are different feelings.

One cannot always gift people with the great outing where they find something so attractive or particular, either because you did not know how to look for the right whale or because she did not want to, but you cannot force them.

As an aside, is this a chance for you to teach? So that what you know will change some people over time and how things are?

I do not hide my way of working. To many captains who were just beginning I explained how I saw the job and how to do it, but very few understand what I say. They keep going after the whales, chasing them. It is something that we need to change.

Does it make it more difficult to have that very connected experience if you have more people on the boat?

Yes, it makes a big difference. First of all, in a small boat I may use a low voice and everyone will listen. If they do not pay attention then I will speak in an even lower voice. On a bigger boat, on the other hand, I have to speak much more loudly, almost yelling. Even if they are all trying to listen, it makes it difficult. No fifty people will be willing to listen at the same time; no fifty people will be willing to look at something at the same time. But fifty people will be anxiously waiting to see the whales, their tails, their breaching—this is what makes it very difficult.

On top of that, the boat that could carry fifty people would be much better for the people to be more comfortable and relaxed if it took only thirty-five. It is perfect on the smaller boats, with just a few people.

You talked about the quiet. One of the things I have noticed when I have gone out is that quite quickly we get to the place where we are all silent. I wonder if you find that with other people, that there is such a sense of awe, that people stop chatting about things.

It is very difficult to compare your outings with the rest. Normally we have to talk about what we are seeing: the callosities on the whale's head, describe the tail, if it is a mother with a baby how much it weighs, how long it is. Then it takes longer to reach the silence.

While going out with you, even if you come with someone who has never seen a whale, we can start by being silent instead of talking about the whales. You begin working in a different way. Also if the whale does not want to come close, you will understand, and I will not feel bad about it.

On a regular outing I have to search for a whale, try for the people to see it close up, and I do not have much time. You are the ones to make the contact. You work!

Are there any other stories that you could share with us, even from other people?

This year on an outing there was a lady who sang, a young whale came up close and as she was singing he would lay on his side, taking his eye from the water to see, most probably to listen as well, since their ear is right behind the eye. There are some studies done about whale sounds and it would be very beautiful for us to be able to make sounds, maybe underwater, because they listen.

On another outing I was watching a mother with her baby. The baby was very sociable, curious, getting close to see the boat while the mom stayed away. The wind moved the boat steadily away from the mom and the baby followed. The distance may have been about nine hundred feet between them, then the mom started calling him by blowing, but the baby kept on coming after the boat. Then she started calling by clapping her pectoral fin against the water and still he remained by the boat.

So now she clapped her tail against the water and this time the baby turned around to go back to her; as he came close she slapped him with her fin! I do not think this was a coincidence.

Do you have any sense, either for you or for other people who have been with the whales that the whales and being with them softens and changes them?

There are some people that have a special contact with animals, these people or me do not always manage to achieve this contact every time, but we respect the animals. We take care of them and we love them.

When I got divorced I was going through a very difficult time in my life. I even thought that I could lose my baby, and I believe the whales helped me a lot. I would get up and be with the problem, go to Piramides and the problem was still there, but when I went out and spent time with the whales the problem was no more. I thought that because I was feeling so bad the whales would not come close, but to the contrary, the whales helped me out.

They are very special.

CHAPTER 42

Facts About Whales— From the Sea Captain

§

THE RIGHT WHALE COMES TO the Valdes Peninsula from June to December. It comes here to give birth, to court and to mate; this is not a feeding area, even though we might see them feeding from time to time.

SOME OF THEIR MOST RELEVANT FEATURES

Head callosities that are exclusively found on Right Whales are used to identify them individually.

No dorsal fin. In this species the pectoral fins have an average length of six feet. The pectoral fin has the same bones that we have in our forearm and fingers; depending on which finger, they will have from six to eight phalanxes per finger.

The caudal peduncle (tail) of an adult female ranges from 12–15 feet in length and has no bones, weighing from 4,000–6,000 pounds; it is what propels the whale forward through vertical movements.

They have two spiracles and the spray produced when they blow is very typical of the species. In the case of the humpbacks for example, even if you see them from up front, you will see only one spurt. The right whale having separate spiracles blows in two clear sprays, whether you see them from the front or the back.

Taking into account that they have lungs, the breathing capacity of a female is around one thousand five hundred liters. When they breath, they ventilate from seventy to ninety percent of that capacity.

VISIBLE DIFFERENCES BETWEEN THE MALE AND FEMALE

The male is slightly smaller than the female, 40–43 feet in length.

Females have around 43–53 feet in length and their weight is 50–55 tons. A female about to give birth weighs around 60–65 tons. The ones that come here to give birth do not mate or participate in the courting groups during that year. It is not known if there is a risk of miscarriage involved.

The main difference between male and female is found on the abdominal region, the male has a genital fold which is longer than the female's, placed close to the navel. Female's genital fold is shorter and placed closer to the anus. Also, the female has two mammary slits, having an internal nipple just as males have internal testis. So if you see just the head and back, unless you can identify them through their callosities or for some special mark in their coloration, you cannot be sure if it is a male or a female whale.

VOCALIZATIONS

These whales do not vocalize as much as the humpbacks do. In humpbacks the vocalizations have a courting purpose, the male sings calling the female. Here, vocalizations are shorter in time and it is unusual to hear them. It occurs sometimes between mothers with young ones, but it is easier to hear the sound of a copulation group, though we do not know who produces them—the female, the males, or all of them.

To vocalize, this species uses two special alveolar sacs that are indirectly communicated to the lungs. The benefit of this is that when it exhales and empties the lungs almost completely, it may still keep on vocalizing with these special sacs. One sac is full of air while the other one is empty, and air flows from one to the other through different ducts. Each duct produces a different series of vibration and therefore different sounds. We may hear some of these sounds but others, waves of a very low frequency, are used for long distance communication and are beyond our hearing capacity. They also use other sounds to communicate, like breaching, clapping their pectoral fins or their flukes against the water. We know very little about their communication.

COMMUNICATION

To give you an example, last year I found orcas following right whales. The whales had grouped together and placed the young ones on the coast side, setting themselves between them and the orcas, defending them with their flukes. The whales remained very close together while the orcas watched from a distance, until they went away. Only then did the whales spread out. What I mean is that there is communication between them but we do not know how it works.

Another example from last year. It was July, a very windy day, when a mother and her young one came over to the boat and bumped against it repeatedly. I could not understand what they were about until I saw a group of orcas close by. As far as I understand it, the young one came towards the boat looking for protection from the orcas.

Also last year there was a Belgian researcher studying whale sounds with a hydrophone. I was fortunate to take her out on the boat to listen to the sounds at night. Boats do not have headlights like cars do and I had to take them to where the whales were. This was a dark night, no moonlight, and we found them. It was amazing how they vocalized! They were mothers with young ones. My feeling, which is not scientific, was that there was one that was calling much more, as if it was a lighthouse under the water. A lighthouse does not shine constantly, it turns on and off, and she was vocalizing in the same way. We do not know at what distance. There were many whales grouped together on one sector of the coast and my belief is that this sound was a way of being alert to a possible predator.

Why did you go out at night?

They went out with us during the day and they had recorded diurnal whale sounds, but they did not know what the whales did at night. For three consecutive nights they went out to record whale sounds. I believe they vocalized more than during the day.

You do not know where the whales go while they are not here?

The whales that have been identified here have been seen in three different feeding grounds. From south to north, the Antarctic sector, the *Orcadas* Islands and the Southern Sandwich Islands with the Georgia Islands, constitute the main feeding grounds. Smaller feeding areas are found by moving eastwards, keeping this same latitude, at the central region of the Atlantic Ocean. There is another more to the north, closer to Brazil's latitude. Also on the central region of the ocean.

The whales that go to South Africa are also Southern Right Whales and feed in the same grounds as ours, so they share the feeding ground and have also been seen mating. It has not yet been demonstrated if the whales who come here go to South Africa too. Considering that some of them have been identified on the coast of Uruguay and Brazil, it is very probable that they would also go there, as they come here on alternate years. Unfortunately there have not been any DNA tests done; that would solve part of the mystery.

CHAPTER 43

Interview with the Nature Preserve Ranger

At The Sea Lion Rookery

§

FOR YOU, WHAT ARE THE whales about?

Now or when I saw them for the first time?

Start with the first time.

We are talking about the '70s in *Punta Norte* (the northern point of the Peninsula Valdes). For me at that time it was basically part of a whole natural system—whales, fauna—it was a natural balance. But what happened is that not just myself but all of us knew very little about whales then, compared to what we know now.

In 1975 I retired and came back here in 1998. At that time I started to see it with different eyes and it has to do with everything that we have heard from people who have been studying them. I believe that their importance is the same if you compare that time and now, but nowadays, knowing more about their life, we see them in a more detailed way.

When you've been with the whales, is there something more beside just what your eyes see?

Not particularly. I don't think so. It is the beauty, the natural, the gigantic—that which is the whale itself. I believe it is part, when one observes one is seeing a balance, a natural balance that at least for me is good to see. The whale in its natural environment.

Why are these whales or the whales important?

It is one of the fundamental pillars of all this Natural Preserve, for sure. One of the fundamental pillars, the Valdes Peninsula itself has its own importance and weight [attraction] with its geography, fauna, sea lions, penguins, terrestrial fauna, plants. But the Whale, its presence, in some way is a layer/stratum that gives more relevance to all of this. I believe that all of this that we have—sea lions, penguins—without the whales, because somehow, even during the season when the whales are not here, like now (due to migration) we are waiting and we know they will arrive. For example, I work with foreign and local tourists. I keep on giving them whale leaflets, like preparing people and making them interested to come back in July or in Spring.

We don't have the Whale here today, but it is very important to know that they will be, that they are going to go and come back again. That is why I, in my job, even when we are out of season I continue to give out the leaflets and such so that people will come back.

I'm happy when I'm here.
  Of course!

For me being with the whales and nature is being with God. For you, and maybe for some of the people who come, is there the same experience?
  For sure! Absolutely. Most people share this. Not just the fauna, things like the sunset we have just seen are very important. Both for the ones who live in a big city but also for me seeing it every day, it is fundamental.

Do you know either for you or for some of the others that come, being in this intense way with nature and God, do you think it changes life or how you are? Or how they live?

Sure, I particularly enjoy my job, being here, being able to transmit all this to visitors with a spectacular, beautiful landscape and a whole natural system where you feel good. I believe that those of us who love this in some way would feel—and maybe I'm a bit exaggerated—but at least I feel the obligation to transmit this.

Thank you for doing so.

CHAPTER 44

Interview with an Argentine Medical Student

§

CAN YOU TELL ME A little bit about what you were thinking before you went, and how the experience was for you in your first encounter with whales?

I didn't know, I went to Piramides to work and I didn't know what I would find there. I remember that we arrived and got immediately on the boat, and made the first outing. As the boat began to go I felt a great emotion and I felt very much like crying. I didn't know why but . . . I didn't understand much. It was as if I had begun to take out the things that were inside of me, like cleansing.

I felt that place was sacred, magic. I kept on crying.

I don't know very well what is it that happened, but there was a turn, a change, a connection, an alignment with my own inner self.

Another of the things that the contact with the whales caused in me was the desire to jump into the water and be with them. If one thinks about that on land you think you are crazy, but in the water (on the boat) that was the feeling I had.

I also found a containment I needed because I was feeling very much alone and I found everyone, even the whales, were holding me.

When you left Piramides and returned to Buenos Aires, were you the same as before you went to the whales or had you become different?

I came back different. I don't know specifically what changed.

In becoming a doctor, what will you do with the schooling that you are receiving? Do you think that this experience will make you at all a different kind of doctor than you would have been without it?

In truth I never thought to be a traditional doctor. My mom always let me see the other side. Since I was small I knew I wanted to be a doctor, but when mom got sick I said I would be a different doctor from the "doctors." I hope I can achieve this.

When you are in Buenos Aires do you think about the whales or feel them, or continue in connection?

I believe that when you come back from Piramides you have a connection that is strong and evident. As time goes by you have it unconsciously. But it is as if they always show up at some point, on a sticker, on a notice, in an article.

Have they shown up at a time when you needed to see them? Was there a correlation between when you've seen something of a whale and something was going on in your life?

Maybe at some point, going by bus I would see. They would turn evident, on a notice or something, and I was filled by the joy, the glow—but only a few times.

If you had one word that you could say about the whales, what would that word be for you?

SALVATION.

Would you like to add another word or leave it there?

Salvation. I believe they help each person, as people have to help them. It is a salvation for the whole world. I believe that the one who manages to connect with them is because she/he wants to save herself to be able to help the rest. It is the truth.

CHAPTER 45

Interview with an Argentine Photographer

§

You are a person who came to live here. When you came, were you already an artist and a photographer?

I knew how to take pictures but I used to work on social events, taking pictures at weddings and schools. I had done some sculpture studies. I was an artist somehow but not as I am now.

I am asking this because I am also interested in how you can talk about this, because you see in a different way than some of us do. Because of the way that you can get inside of what is and show it. I am very interested in hearing about your beginnings with the whales and how it is for you now.

So can you start with when you first came, when you first saw the whales, how this began for you?

In 1999, after living for two years at the capital, I returned to my mother's house to think where I wanted to continue with my life. I thought about Bariloche, in the mountains where I was born, I thought about Puerto Piramide, where I had a friend who had come two years earlier. So I decided to make a trip to both places to decide where was it that I could continue my life.

In Bariloche I met a photographer, and we are friends now, but that is where we met. It was at a photography developing lab that I saw he was taking pictures of condors. He was at the counter by my side and my brother introduced us. We talked for five or ten minutes and he asked me, "How do you relate to nature?" I did not know how answer.

He invited me to visit the condors because he believed I would be respectful. A week before arriving here and meeting the whales I started to think about this issue of relating to nature; I had been with the condors.

When we arrived in Puerto Piramide, the cliffs and their timelessness blew me away. Now I understand it was that what hit me so much. At that time I did not know what I was feeling.

From my first whale-watch outing what I remember is that from all the explanations that were given on board I was astounded by the time. I kept hearing this phrase, "millions of years."

Today I believe that they are under the water and when they come up they come into our reality. It is as if they are there, I do not see them, but they are and then they come up. That is what I recall from those first encounters. This being a part of reality, coming into it and being a part of it. Today what I understand is that I am a part of that reality, but when I arrived I felt just as an observer of that reality. I believe that what I lived with the whales was precisely that "feeling a part of."

Have you had any particular time when the whales have been with you in a way that was strong?

Yes, of course!

Can you tell me?

Yes, like right now. [This interview took place immediately following the outing described in The Eye, Chapter 29.] That would be first. If I have to search my memory for something like that, I think it has more to do with my own receptivity than with what they may show or do.

Has that changed from when you first came to now, your receptivity?

Yes, now I let them do whatever they want to do. Let's say, before I might want them to do something of my choice, rather than what they wanted. Sometimes it is strange because instead of thinking the most about what they are giving me, I center more in what I can give to them. I could say that I tighten my stomach or something, searching for a way, believing I can also emit. I do not doubt of what they emit.

We were talking this afternoon and you were saying some wise words. I wonder if you could tell someone who wanted to know what you have learned and seen, what would you tell him or her?

Every day I go on the boat with seventy people and try to find an agreement.

You talked this afternoon at lunch about a word that you had discovered that was part of what you have learned. I wonder if you could talk about that now.

First of all, the word was "Evolutionary," because evolution is a more abstract concept, like something separate from us. But today I wrote Evolutionary, because it seemed the best way to describe the whales. It is hard for me to express what they are for me in a different way.

A week ago a magazine requested I talk about myself. I talked about my relationship with the whales, not about myself. It was very much related to this talk we are having now, words flowed. The first words I wrote were, "When I arrived I felt attracted by them, trapped by them and touched."

After that I tried to describe them and what came up is that concept "evolutionary beings." They are the little drops that fell "ping, ping, ping" for millions of years, the drops that they are is a lot. I had never heard or seen that word before, or noticed its importance. What an evolutionary being may bring and how important it is for myself to believe in my own evolution. Because not every change has to be shocking or traumatizing; instead they may come about through constancy, discipline, but mostly though the "ping, ping, ping."

That is very beautiful!
I cannot tell this to everyone.

Since we are here and we are not everyone, is there anything else that you can talk about with us?
As human beings we are a genus and it seems to me that each one of us who knows today a reality with whales has to carry the debate of what it means to conserve them. We have to start to imagine the year 3000 with whales because the only way for it to become a reality is for us to start thinking of it. Until yesterday I had never thought of a future with whales and that is, I believe, the first sin I have committed, not to think about a future with whales.

In truth I believe I tried two times to think about a future with whales, because even working here it seems they are already condemned to disappear, and it does not have to be like that. I believe we should all start to close our eyes and believe in a possible future; that is how it will be possible. It would be a mistake not to conserve this for those who come after us.

What I tell passengers every day is that for our generation, the particular case of the whales is where the difference lies in whether we fulfill the aims we are here to achieve or not. The subject we are here to attend has a strong indicator in the whales, it seems to me. "Which reality are we leaving for those who come after us?" We are one genus, we have made many mistakes, and we do not know what is coming. But what will come is in our hands, it depends on us. It depends on us if there will be whales or not. It depends on us if our children's great-grandchildren will feel through computer and science or through reality. It seems the challenge and the beauty of all that is coming is in what we humans do, everything related to urban settings, and we are forgetting to relate to nature. As I have heard somewhere that Mother Nature, if we do not learn to relate with her in a different way, she will reject us. We are running counterclockwise, before it is too late. I wish that instead of the five of us, we were five hundred people talking about this and some day we will do it. Otherwise we do not succeed in our commitment and this is not for us.

The only thing we have to do is hold a microphone and talk to those seventy people on the boat. They are on holidays and do not want to talk about conservation, nature, or anything of the sort. But when I end up talking, if one or two of them will talk someday to someone else about what we have shared and what I mentioned, that is what I have to think about. If they did what I would like them to do at the time, they would start to cry! To be able to deal with this we have to hold on to hope.

(As the biologist translator begins to cry with tears choking her voice, another translator takes over and says, "It is as if we met you when you were looking for hope and did not know where it was. Now you are a carrier of hope.")

Your wisdom and what you know and what you can tell is real.

I do not know if you really understand this. For me you are multiplying agents, agents of change, of the argument I can rise when on the boat, when confronting seventy people, five times a day.

Every day, they [the whales] are there, they are queens. There are a lot of people that come motivated by a different mechanism. Their decision is between going skiing, going wherever, or coming to see the whales. However unknowingly they *feel*. I see seventy hearts open on every trip. Many times people do not realize what is going on, they think it is just because. In these last six months of going out every day, there was never a time when a person would come to tell me how awful it was, or that they did not feel anything at all.

This continuing to be close, it makes me happy. I am happy that there are others who want to remain close and keep coming, because then it takes on a different dimension. It would be unfair to expect that from the person who comes for just an hour of whale watching, they have a different experience.

I want to say a very deep thank you for who you are.

CHAPTER 46

Interview with an Owner of a Whale Watching Company/Sea Captain

§

How did you get involved with the whales? What brought you here?

Adventure. I was very young, seventeen. I had no will or reason to study, or do anything. I was living in Buenos Aires where the situation at that time was very difficult. My parents also wanted to leave. This was around 1977; we were in the midst of practically a civil war. Actually the situation was I got kicked out of my last year in senior high school and I had either to confront my parents with the situation or run away. So I ran away.

I came here, where I had been on vacation and had met some divers and I wanted to be a diver. If I had told them (my parents) that I would be a diver, it was impossible, so that is how I ended up straight here.

I'm going to back up so that we have on the tape what you told me earlier about your family.

My mother is from the East Coast in the States, from a very, very old family. My grandfather on my mother's side graduated from Yale's school of law. My grandfather on my father's side also graduated from La Sorbonne. Background has nothing to do if you compare it to this, but what may be interesting is some values that have been passed down in the family. We sometimes feel that we are very old fashioned in some ways, in certain things, but actually I think that our societies in the last fifty years, have been looking for success more than other things. For my father it was more important to be a gentleman still, than something else. Even though he was a fisherman, a sheep ranger, a wine maker, he graduated as a system's analyst engineer. What is very interesting is that you would say because of his background he would have in some ways conditioned us, but actually it was not like that for any of us. I have five brothers and two sisters and none of us have been conditioned.

So you arrived to be a diver here in Piramides.
Actually in Madryn and then I went to live in San Jose in a trailer and then, about eight months later, my father decided to move the whole family and join us and be together in this whole thing.

So we ended up living in the other gulf in a place about 40 km from here called El Riacho. There was a ranch there and two other small houses and that is where we decided to build a house which today is the school of the place. We donated it to the province and they made the school. It is very nice, because most of it we built with our own hands. Between the brothers and my father, we put the layers of bricks, fixed the windows and floors, and today it is a school.

From that how did you end up here owning the whale watching company?
We already had the boats, we were fishing divers, and people would come and ask, "Can we go see the whales?" Then I met Mariano and started to work with him as an employee. That was for eight or nine years. I would sometimes take my own boat, not work with Mariano for two months and then go fishing, or diving. Also I would take people

diving as a tourist-operator or take foreigners and Europeans in a fishing boat. Then whale-watching started demanding more and more time; it started to grow and to be successful and I got into this.

Finally about twelve years ago we sat down with Mariano and talked about the option of going into a partnership with it. And that is how it started.

So for you is this a business only or is there something that pulls or calls to you, with the whales?

I think it has to do . . . business is an accessory really to what the main reason, why it adds to the concept of adventure as I said before. The sense of adventure, or having an adventurous life, an adrenaline type of activity, is very different from just having a traditional type of activity. It has to do with the sense of openness towards what is around you and taking, practicing that. It is in a way spiritual. It has to do with the atmosphere and you have to not let it die.

So the business was successful, OK, perfect! I worked for that too. But if I did not have the business I would be in the water the same. I would be in the same environment. I love this area, and I love the animals. I really do not care too much if I will be wealthy or not, compared to that. It is something different that pushes you on into this life.

That answers my question beautifully and I am not surprised by what you say.

So you go out in the water and you are in this magnificent place in Creation and you watch people as well as watch the whales. Do you have any experiences that stand out in your mind with people or . . . ?

Yes, I think every time and every trip, you share the joy or the emotions of people who are strongly moved or the peacefulness that comes to people. Each trip is unique and that is one of the things if you look at it. I have been working for 27 years with people, going out every day;

there is a routine in it. But what makes the whole difference—and I haven't much experience in other jobs so I really don't know well what is routine for other people. Here you are dealing with subtly different situations, every day, and every trip.

You have always different people, weather conditions, the sea conditions, the whales are different, even if they are the same whales. Their behavior is different. How everything interrelates or weaves together is very interesting. I think in a way it becomes a whole picture. If you look at a whale-watching trip it is not that, "Oh! We had really bad weather, it was a disaster." You find that some people will work things out in themselves totally different, what the weather is offering them, whether they are suffering, or what is happening, what is out there. Everything has to do with this picture of what you are living in life.

You are really living very unique situations every time.

Is the experience different with children, older people, people from different countries?

It is always different no matter what. I have had two great trips that I always remember. One was a trip for handicapped children and there were two blind girls on board. Of course, they could hear the whales and the other sense available for them was touch. The whale lifted and put her fluke up above them, everybody tried to touch them but the fluke was right above the girls, and they had water falling on them. They were just touching on top of their heads. Something that weighs between five and six thousand pounds. That experience for me is the experience of my lifetime in this activity.

And there are other situations. There was a French Soul and Blues singer who came and she was heartbroken. She was beautiful, rich, talented, everything. And she was heartbroken. She came here on vacation just by chance. She went out one time and liked it and came to the office to ask how much it would cost her to go out on every single trip for a week. She came up to me and said, "I really feel like singing to them. What do you think about it?" I said it was fine and she went to the stern of the boat, sat there, and started to sing to two passing whales. They stopped, turned around, came towards her and stood there, and three more joined in. We had five whales around us, paying attention to her. She sang for forty-five minutes and they stayed all that time. Everybody was moved. My sister was working with me at the time and she was crying, she was very emotional.

Another time we went out with the Native shaman after Afghanistan was invaded and the boat was full of people. We sang a pipe song, gave tobacco to everybody, and there was a chorus aboard who sang the *Angelus* and that was beautiful, very nice. I think those were times that were very, very. . . .

I have had people who had been very sick and had just "steadied" and were so grateful to life, for that! And I am not saying that's all they said. They were so grateful to life. Maybe they were feeling miserable about other things but that moment there was . . . so it was very good.

You also do worldwide work with whales. You were in Japan.

Yes, I was in Japan, in Iceland, in Uruguay, Brazil, and Chile.

Can you tell me about what you are doing What's happening and what we can be doing?

I have been helping whale-watching organizations and they have a very strong stand regarding whale hunting. They have many projects regarding animal welfare, not only with wild animals also domestics.

In this case, having this business in this area being so successful economically, has affected the life of this whole town and many people around the area like Madryn and Trelew (towns by the sea in Patagonia) so positively. I go around providing know-how in developing places of whale watching, especially in countries that have a national policy for whale hunting, specifically Japan and Iceland, where the national policy is pro-whaling. I have been supporting the development of whale watching, as it is much more intelligent to be able to see a whale, hundreds and thousands of times than it is to eat it all at once.

Is this progressing?

There was this congress in Japan. There were about fourteen operators, some of which had been working for about fifteen years, but their businesses have never been able to develop. The congress was in a place called Kochi last year. It is one of the largest fishing ports, compared to other cities in Japan it is a small city, 90 km from Tokyo, so it is pretty close by.

They started three years ago there, sperm whale watching and dolphin watching. It is an area that is a feeding ground for sperm whales; it is one of the prime fishing grounds also for the Japanese for centuries. Actually the dock was built in the 1650; it is really very interesting.

The idea was to provide from our experience, what we had done, how we had dealt with certain problems. Whale watching is very complex because you have to take care, very much, of the animals, because they are sustaining the whole texture of your activity around them. So you have to teach the people involved directly into it, a series of techniques we have developed towards understanding the behavior of the whales towards boats, and this is very, very difficult. You have to train actually to get the skill, and it has to be somebody who is gifted, otherwise it takes some years to develop that sensitivity towards whale behavior. All this is what we try to share and to transmit to other people in other places.

There is also the reality that well, this—Piramides—was a town of sixty people, twenty years ago and there was nothing. No electricity, nothing. And how whale watching has benefited the community and has improved the quality of life of this community. Having electricity in Japan is very normal but imagine a place way out of the way, which is kind of the farthest places you can imagine in the world, and to be able to have that type of development in those ways is very important.

To back up to the training of the people, because there is some conversation around the whale-watching industry. How much does it harass the whales and how is that to be handled? I think it is important what you are telling me and what you are telling people elsewhere.

It happens also that always when there is money involved things get twisted a little bit here and a little bit there. That is one of the things that we want to really work into, trying to be fair for everybody, for the different businesses but also and most important of all, to be very careful and very cautious with the whales. You have to limit; you have to regulate things because of this situation with money. Maybe in the States it does not happen but here you have a lot of corruption in the society and especially in politicians.

I have to say again that I am glad you hold the place that you do for this community and for the world.

Since you have been here in all of these years, what have you seen with numbers of whales? Have they come back, their babies?

Actually we have had a very strong come back of the population in these last years. Thirty years ago there were very few animals; we have been seeing these in the last years. But also there are changes that have to do with the things that we do.

There is so little that we understand that really it would take many years to be able to get a general picture. Even though one is positive and you think, "OK, there have been eighty or a hundred calves this year." But our capacity as humans to create chaos is huge, and maybe just because we'll start developing this new ranch or we'll start mining for gold or mercury, or maybe the aluminum plant will start using a new technology using PCBs. The whales are still so outnumbered because they are so few.

One thing that is interesting about the ocean is that we look at the ocean as infinite, and it is maybe for our eyes, it is. But in the real sense it is very, very, very delicate. It is even more delicate than the earth, especially in what regards pollution.

So from very few what is the Southern Right Whale population now?
Around three thousand.

So you and others are working and paying attention to these potential risks and threats.
Luckily, in general the whole community has a very informed view of these aspects. There are a number of NGOs associated for this and taking part in it, so there is a lot of public opinion involved in many of these issues. Still in Argentina there is a very strong public opinion, but it is not as well developed as in other countries. This is recent history in this way.

So you are a pioneer in this?
Yes, you could say that.

You took us out on a trip a few days ago that was very beautiful and powerful; can you talk about it some from your perspective?
I feel absolutely privileged and blessed by the whole picture. It is very difficult to say how unique this situation is. I am so lucky just being

there, and I feel very blessed by that. It sounds very detached from that experience but the thing is that for me it is the whole thing.

I will give back some words that you gave to us. We were watching mating groups and the words that you gave us were . . .

> *The Art of Love*
> *Where it all begins The Hand of God.*

I say thank you to you for these beautiful words, for bringing us to that place where we could see and be part of the Art of Love, the Beginning, and the Hand of God. Thank you.
Thank God!

And Thank God is what this is all about.
Exactly.

CONCLUSION

§

Ask, and it will be given to you;
seek, and you will find;
knock, and it will be opened to you.

MATTHEW 7:7

I HAVE WRITTEN MY STORY and compiled the writings and interviews of others so that their stories can also be documented. We tell of a longing for meaning, for a different world where freedom, compassion, and social justice exist. In this longing, we heard a call to the whales. Creation in Her divine embrace heard our cry and answered. We asked and we found. In the years I have been going to the whales I have observed lives changing significantly after deep connection to the whales.

This listening to the whales and opening to Creation has encouraged people, sometimes gently, sometimes dramatically, to evolve and transform. Answers to questions have been heard and a radiant opening to the Divine experienced. Strong threads have emerged, threads of being powerfully loved and seen, of melting into sacred energy, cherishing Creation, receiving wisdom, shedding unnecessary encumbrances, becoming free, opening to creativity, and learning to stand up and speak out. People have returned to school and have discovered new work. It has been a pilgrimage filled with intense inner work, awe, prayer, ritual, joy, and gratitude. As we dance with Creation we become more fully the divine selves that we are. We then become what we were created to be in the world.

Direct observation is very clear. Each of us who speaks in this book knows that our lives have indeed been blessed by transformation, a gift we received from opening to the embrace of the whales and Creation in Patagonia.

The Call

§

Tell me, what is it you plan to do
with your one wild and precious life?

—MARY OLIVER[50]

NOW IN 2017 AS I reflect on my time with the whales in Argentina I am filled with awe and enormous gratitude. I realize once again the blessing I received from the whales and Creation and all of the people I encountered who walked with me on this surprising mystical adventure.

This beautiful experience which began in the year 2000 became a sacred pilgrimage of healing and the discovery of mystical love. My experience blasted open who I thought I was. Having been told who and how I should be and what I should do by my culture, I did not realize that there was an authentic interior longing to be free. I think this is true for many of us. The absoluteness of society is strong. The whales pierced through that covering with a teaching that I was not alone, I was being guided by the Divine and that within me there is a unique Divine core. I was shown who I was called to be rather than who civilization told me I should be. This was a joyous discovery experienced with the whales and with all of Creation. It is the purpose of a Sacred Encounter.

However, this was only the first step on a mystical journey. The second step is bringing the experience into the world. The writing and publication of this book is a part of that second step. May my telling of our stories be worthy of the gift we received and an inspiration for the call to learn from, protect, love, and dance with Creation. If we who speak in this book, all of us ordinary people, can be impacted by a sacred encounter, it is indeed possible for everyone.

It is even more imperative today to open to divine inspiration in this world desperately in need of compassion, social justice, and action. We must listen to the cries of the world. We can no longer be complacent, quiet, or insecure. We have work to do.

We must act.

Mysticism, the magnificent direct experience of God, requires this return to action. We see even more clearly the critical importance of respecting, honoring, and caring for all of life. The power of Creation opened me so that I could tell our story and become more effective and committed in the world. I returned to my work with a deep reverence for the earth, an expanded global awareness supporting and honoring all religions, and a vow to continue the work of building a safety net of opportunity and love for vulnerable and suffering people.

Where does one find a sacred encounter? Listen to the words of the faith traditions. Pray with them. And remember Creation speaks in all of Her ways. The glorious transformative and healing call for me was in South America with the whales. For you perhaps it will be a tree, the forest, the mountains, the desert, the sea, the stars, a wolf, an eagle or . . . ?

Sacred encounters are available. The search is universal, to be healed and live a life of meaning and service. Many of us struggle, asking where and how we can help. Nature is one of the ways waiting to heal us and teach us. We can listen right here, right now, in nature, open in prayer, in meditation. Sit with Her. Be with Her. Pay attention. You will hear your unique call. There are a myriad of places crying, needing, longing for our time, our dollars, and our skills.

We can be love and skill in action.

We are needed.

NOTES

1. Andrew Harvey, *The Essential Mystics: The Soul's Journey into Truth* (New Jersey: Castle Books, 1996) p. 6.

2. Mary Oliver, *New and Selected Poems* (Boston: Beacon Press, 1992) p. 114.

3. Jean Houston, *Jump Time* (Boulder: Sentient Publications, 2004) p. 7.

4. Viktor E. Frankl, *Man's Search for Meaning,* translated by Ilse Lasch (New York: Simon and Schuster, 1962) p. 97.

5. Matthew Fox, *Creation Spirituality* (New York: HarperSanFrancisco, 1991) p.75.

6. Alfredo Lichter and Claudio Campagna, *On the Shores of a Cold Sea River: Nature on Patagonian Coasts* (Puerto Madryn, Argentina: Fundacion EcoCentro, 2000) p. 7.

7. Gloria Durka, *Praying with Hildegard of Bingen* (Winona, MN: Saint Mary's Press, 1991) p. 32.

8. Frank Stewart, ed., *The Presence of Whales* (Anchorage: Alaska Northwest Books, 1995) p. 294.

9. Bill Plotkin, *Soulcraft* (Novato, CA: New World Library, 2003) p. 237.

10. Robert A. Johnson, *Ecstasy* (San Francisco: HarperSanFrancisco, 1989) p. 24.

11. Thich Nhat Hanh, CD, *Teachings on Love,* read by the author (Sounds True, 2004).

12. Fred Graham, *The Whale,* wooden sculpture (Seattle: The Burke Museum, 2004).

13. Matthew Fox, *Original Blessing* (Santa Fe, NM: Bear and Company, 1983) p. 69.

14. Jamie Sams and David Carson, *Medicine Cards* (Santa Fe, NM: Bear and Company, 1988) p. 201.

15. Sams, p. 202.

16. Jessica Dawn Palmer, *Animal Wisdom* (London: Element/HarperCollins, 2002) p. 365.

17. Andrew Harvey, *The Essential Mystics: The Soul's Journey into Truth* (Edison, New Jersey: Castle Books, 1996) p. 4.

18. Matthew Fox, *Meditations with Meister Eckhart* (Santa Fe, NM: Bear and Company, 1983) p. 110.

19. Matthew Fox, *Creation Spirituality* (New York: HarperSanFrancisco,1991) p. 30.

20. Marion Woodman with Jill Mellick, *Coming Home to Myself* (Berkeley: Conari Press, 1998) p. 46.

21. Alexandra Morton, *Listening to Whales: What the Orcas Have Taught Us* (New York: Ballantine Books, 2004) p. 138.

22. Lao-tsu, *Tao te Ching*, translated by Gia-fu Feng and Jane English (New York: Vintage Books, 1989) p. 18.

23. Scott Taylor, *Souls in the Sea: Dolphins, Whales and Human Destiny* (Berkeley: Frog, Ltd., 2003) p. 6.

24. Robert Bly, *The Kabir Book* (Boston: A Seventies Press Book, 1977) p. 24.

25. Coleman Barks, trans., with John Moyne, A. J. Arberry, Reynold Nicholson, *The Essential Rumi* (Edison, NJ: Castle Books, 1997) p. 36.

26. Don Campbell, *The Mozart Effect* (New York: Avon Books, 1997) p. 31.

27. Layne Redmond, *When the Drummers Were Women* (New York: Three Rivers Press, 1997) p. 12.

28. Robert Gass with Kathleen Brehony, *Chanting: Discovering Spirit in Sound* (New York: Broadway Books, 1999) flyleaf.

29. Matthew Fox, *Creation Spirituality* (New York: HarperSanFrancisco, 1991) p. 10.

30. David R. Hawkins, M.D., Ph.D., *Power vs. Force: The Hidden Determinants of Human Behavior* (Carlsbad, CA: Hay House, 2005) pp. 272–273.

31. Roger Payne, *Among Whales* (New York: Delta/Dell Publishing, 1995) p. 327.

32. Payne, p. 122.

33. Matthew Fox, *A Spirituality Named Compassion: Uniting Mystical Awareness with Social Justice* (Rochester, VT: Inner Traditions, 1999) p. 150.

34. Thomas Berry, *The Dream of the Earth* (San Francisco: Sierra Club Books, 1990) p. 211.

35. Witi Ihimaera, *The Whale Rider* (Orlando, FL: Harcourt, Inc., 2003) p. 150.

36. Brian Swimme, *The Hidden Heart of the Cosmos: Humanity and the New Story* (New York: Orbis Books, 1998) p. 45.

37. Larry Dossey, M.D., *Recovering the Soul: A Scientific and Spiritual Search* (New York: Bantam Books, 1989) p. 271.

38. Shaina Noll, *Songs for the Inner Child* (Singing Heart Productions, 1992) CD 1.

39. Bill Grace, *The Seattle Times,* 15 September 2005, B9.

40. Andrew Harvey, *Light Upon Light: Inspirations from Rumi* (Berkeley: North Atlantic Books, 1996) p. 69.

41. Mircea Eliade, *Rites and Symbols of Initiation: The Mysteries of Birth and Rebirth,* translated by Willard R. Trask (Woodstock, CT: Spring Publications, 1995) p. 64.

42. Thomas Berry, *The Dream of the Earth* (San Francisco: Sierra Club Books, 1990) p. 134.

43. Barbara G. Walker, *The Woman's Dictionary of Symbols and Sacred Objects* (New York: HarperSanFrancisco, 1988) p. 200.

44. Scott Taylor, *Souls in the Sea: Dolphins, Whales and Human Destiny* (Berkeley: Frog, Ltd., 2003) p. 6.

45. Matthew Fox, *Meditations with Meister Eckhart* (Santa Fe, NM: Bear and Company, 1983) p. 21.

46. Thomas E. Mails, *Fools Crow: Wisdom and Power* (Tulsa: Council Oak Books, 1991) p. 36.

47. Peter Felix Kellermann and M. K. Hudgins, *Psychodrama with Trauma Survivors* (London: Jessica Kingsley Publishers, 2001) p. 13.

48. Leonard Peltier, *Prison Writing: My Life is My Sun Dance* (New York: St. Martin's Press, 1999) p. 216).

49. Henry D. Thoreau, *Walden* (Princeton: Princeton University Press, 1973) p. 326.

50. Mary Oliver, *New and Selected Poems* (Boston: Beacon Press, 1992) p. 94.

51. Matthew Fox, *Meditations with Meister Eckhart* (Santa Fe, NM: Bear and Company, 1983) p. 34.

ACKNOWLEDGMENTS

§

ENORMOUS GRATITUDE TO THE REVEREND Jerry Hanna for introducing me to meditation and blessing me with his wise spiritual guidance and teachings through the years.

Love to Dorothy Walters for her exquisite sacred poetry and for her relentless insistence that I publish this book, and for her friendship.

To Shirley Barclay, gifted shaman and medicine woman who initiated me into Native American prayer, healing, and rituals, and for taking me to the whales in Argentina.

To Monica Zuretti for the beauty of her welcome to Argentina and for teaching me South American ways, showing me the interaction of psychodrama and the whales and for her help and encouragement in writing this book.

To Paula Echaniz for walking the whale journey with me and for her magnificent ability to translate for all of us and to Juliana, Paula's daughter, who brought a child's innocence to the early days.

To Matthew Fox for opening my eyes to the wonder of Creation Spirituality.

To Andrew Harvey for blasting my heart open to the Beloved and for his powerful passion for Sacred Activism.

To Clarissa Pinkola Estes for teaching courage and the importance of Original Voice.

To Jenny D'Angelo for her editing, enthusiasm, and support, and for her love of the whales.

To the late whale elder Mariano and to Sergio, Rafa and Angel who brought the wisdom of the whales alive.

For all of the people who wrote their stories or were interviewed giving the myriad of experiences with the whales a voice.

For my children Katie, Amy, and Michael for their support and help with this book, their wonderful spouses and magnificent grandchildren for their love and being bringers of joy.

Huge appreciation once again for my husband Jon, the Argentine people who embraced me, and the Southern Right Whales for their beauty, magnificence, wisdom, and love.

THANK YOU

§

If the only prayer
You say in your entire life
Is "Thank You"
That would suffice.

—Meister Eckhart[51]

Gracias

Gracias

Gracias

Fig. 11. A Southern Right Whale

70367977R00105

Made in the USA
San Bernardino, CA
28 February 2018